Gorge Justice

RUSTY BRADSHAW

Copyright © 2021 Rusty Bradshaw
All rights reserved
First Edition

PAGE PUBLISHING, INC.
Conneaut Lake, PA

First originally published by Page Publishing 2021

ISBN 978-1-6624-4468-5 (pbk)
ISBN 978-1-6624-4469-2 (digital)

Printed in the United States of America

This book is dedicated to my mother, Phyllis Shattuck. That summer spent with her in the Columbia River Gorge inspired this story.

Chapter 1

Visiting the Columbia River Gorge was something Sherry had always wanted to do again.

She had traveled down it once before when she was seven years old. Even at that age, she had retained the memories. She recalled how enraptured she was at the scenery.

Formed over millions of years of erosion and at least one Ice Age, the river originates in the Rocky Mountains of British Columbia, Canada. It begins its journey going northwest but shortly turns south, slicing through the state of Washington. The waterway turns west near Kennewick, Washington, and a few miles later, it forms the border between Washington and the state of Oregon. The river eventually empties into the Pacific Ocean on the North Oregon Coast.

The river is a study in contrast when it makes the turn west. For a number of miles, the high cliffs on each side are nearly barren of vegetation. About a third of the way to the coast, the high banks start to sprout trees and brush of varying types. Farther downstream, the cliffs are covered with them.

It was that contrast that mesmerized Sherry all those years ago. She always wanted to go back. Now she was, but for all the wrong reasons.

Sherry was moving from the small Wyoming town that had been her home all her life up to now. There was something she had to get away from.

The previous year, she had gotten pregnant. Small towns being what they are, the fact would get out sooner or later. Sherry's grandmother, her father's mother, who had lived there much of her life, had a saying about the town.

"If you go for a walk in the woods, not only would everyone in town know by the time you got back but the gossip would have twisted the story to say that you screwed a bear while you were out there," she said to her children and grandchildren a number of times.

Sherry's parents were prominent members of the community, volunteering for nearly every activity in the small mountain community. The area was also old school in its moral outlook, at least in the public eye. While residents, especially the older generation, held others to a high standard, there was plenty of questionable behavior practiced behind closed doors.

To save the family any public embarrassment, Sherry's parents helped her get an abortion in Colorado. This was all done in secret, of course. But true to her grandmother's description of the town, secrets are hard to keep in small towns, and it leaked out.

Sherry Dyke was still in high school—just completed her junior year—and she didn't want to leave school. But there was plenty of judgment from the adults in the community and some from her schoolmates. The worst treatment came from the boys in high school, who nearly all now saw her as easy. Plenty made sexual advances toward her and were angry when she refused them.

It had not gone to the point of violence, but all that happened after the abortion was too much for her to handle.

Sherry was not the only target of the community's scorn. One by one, they began to see their friends turn against them, and they found their volunteer efforts were not appreciated. Sherry's younger siblings who were still at home were also the targets of ridicule from their classmates.

So when school was completed, the family packed up and moved to Washington.

Sherry's father had connections in the logging industry in a small town called Carson, just a few miles north of the Columbia River. In addition to a job, he secured the family a house.

With all that still fresh in her mind, Sherry was working to put it behind her and focus on what lay ahead. A new home and a chance to start over beckoned. She was eager to answer the call.

As the family's 1970 Chevrolet Impala station wagon glided down the Washington side of the river on the windy two-lane State Highway 14, she watched the countryside roll by. It reminded her of a storybook place. It all seemed too beautiful to be true.

Born and raised in Wyoming's mountains, Sherry was awed by their majesty. But they never did measure up, in her mind, to the Columbia River Gorge she remembered from her youth. The Gorge at this point in the journey had its own high mountains, but they were separated by a majestic large river.

Many years ago, the river was like most with fast-moving water and rapids and waterfalls scattered along its length. But man's technological advancements had changed that.

Starting in British Columbia, engineers had constructed fourteen dams on the river to generate hydroelectric power and for irrigation. Of those structures, the final four are in the Gorge. The water backed up behind each dam, eliminated the winding route of the river and the rapids, and created a body of water that at most points in the Gorge was at least one mile wide. It looked more like an elongated lake.

Sherry knew she was going to like it here.

The blue Chevy station wagon passed by a large lumber mill alongside the river near the very small town of Home Valley. While the distinctive semitractor log trucks were unloading in the mill yard, there were logs tied up in large bunches in the river itself. This was so different from the way it was done in the mountains of Wyoming, where the practice of floating logs from the forests down the river through her hometown to the mills along the way had gone out of style many years ago.

Seeing the logs in the river gave Sherry an appreciation for history.

That very mill was where her father would be working. It was larger than the mill in her former Wyoming home.

At the western edge of Home Valley, where the main highway continued along the river's edge, they crossed a bridge over the mouth of the Wind River, where it emptied into Columbia, then turned right onto a road that eventually turned into Hot Spring Avenue that split through the south end of Carson. It was along that road her father steered the car. The terrain looked vaguely familiar, and she knew she had been here on that trip ten years before.

As they drove into Carson itself, the familiarity remained, but it was more intense. That was because it was similar to the town in which she had spent her whole life, up to this point. When they pulled up to the new house on Smith Beckon Road, Sherry liked it immediately.

The house was large. It had to be. The Dykes had five children. Terry was the oldest at nineteen. He had joined the Navy the year before, and after eight weeks of boot camp at Great Lakes Naval Training Center in Michigan, he was stationed to the Puget Sound Naval Shipyard in Seattle. Next came Sherry at seventeen, Mary at fourteen, and Ralph at thirteen. Kim, at ten, was the youngest. Bob and Katrina had been married nineteen years—it would be twenty in October. Each year had been happy ones for them.

Maybe that was why the Dyke children got along better than kids in other families they knew. They were all very close, with no cliques, like in some large families. And they all stuck up for one another, no matter the problem.

With that kind of closeness, it did not take them long to unload the cramped wagon and the U-Haul trailer it towed. They had packed in the car and trailer only the essentials; the rest was on its way in a tractor trailer moving truck, which was more than an hour behind them on the road.

With the car and trailer unloaded, Sherry and Mary, with their parents' permission, went to explore the town. The older sisters, because they were the first two girls in the family, were the closest emotionally of the siblings. They knew each other's secrets—all of them. In fact, when Sherry discovered she was pregnant, Mary was the first one she told.

Mary was also the only one Sherry initially told who the father of the baby would have been had it been born. But Bob and Katrina, along with Sherry's other siblings, were to find out through the small-town grapevine. Once that secret was known around town, the prospective father began to harass Sherry and her family.

Another reason the sisters were so close was because their interests were almost identical. Most of what they did was done together. Once Mary began to date last year, they even double-dated.

Sherry had taken advantage of her parents' understanding nature when it came to her pregnancy. She also knew she had an ace in the hole whenever her parents began talking to her about getting sexually involved at her age. Terry was conceived before her parents were married, and any time they began to talk about her pregnancy, she pointed that out to them. That always ended the conversation.

It wasn't that Bob and Katrina were permissive. They simply felt like hypocrites trying to lecture their daughter against something they had done.

But now that the trouble of the pregnancy and abortion was seemingly behind her, Sherry wanted to forget it and everything connected with it. She had told her parents she wanted to get away from that town and the people who had judged her, ridiculed her. She wanted a fresh start.

Because the family was so close, and because people in the small Wyoming town also focused their wrath on the parents, it was an easy sell. Bob had enough connections that getting another job and making the move financially was easy. Katrina, though she had never completed her post-high school education because of her own premarital pregnancy, had skills as a nurse and had worked in several jobs, including waitressing and tending bar, so getting work elsewhere would not be a problem. Because the siblings were so close, none objected to the move to protect their sister, and their parents, from what they saw as unfair treatment.

They were all strong, flexible, and resilient. They knew they could make the adjustment.

Sherry and Mary wanted to be back to help with further unloading, so they made a quick walk north on Smith Beckon Road, turning west. They noticed a fabric and clothing store a block north on Barnes Road. They continued west to Wind River Road then turned south. They saw two general stores. That was the extent of it in that general area, but what they saw was interesting and worth more exploration. They made mental notes of shops they wanted to revisit, then they completed a square home by going east on Hot Springs Road and north on Smith Beckon Road back to the house.

When they got back to the house, the moving truck was there and unloading was underway. The movers and their father were busy bringing in large items, and their mother gave them the task of getting the smaller items put away as dressers and other furniture came in.

The Dykes' new house in Carson was a simple two-story box-style structure No two houses in Carson were alike in exterior or floor plan appearance There were no cookie-cutter developments, just singular homes built to suit their first owners' desires.

On the outside, the house certainly looked lived in. The main forest-green paint scheme with the light-gray trim was in need of a coat or two. There were several spots, mostly on the trim boards, where sections would need to be replaced before the repainting.

There was a covered porch the length of the front of the house. It was clear this was a fairly new addition as the wood was in better shape. But the builder did not paint it to match the house; it was still bare wood that had not been varnished or sealed. The wet Gorge weather had already started to take its toll. Bob planned to remedy that as soon as possible.

Inside, the four-bedroom house included a large living room, a breakfast nook, a kitchen, three bathrooms, and a den, which was to be set up as the family room. That was where the television would be, along with the large collection of books and board games.

The living and family rooms were separated from the kitchen by walls, with connecting doors. One bathroom was downstairs. There was a large room at the back of the house that included hookups for a washer and dryer, and there was a large industrial-looking sink in the room as well.

Being the oldest girl, Sherry could easily have claimed a bedroom to herself. However, she and Mary wanted to share a room. With Terry already out of the house, that allowed Ralph and Kim, as the youngest children, the opportunity to have their own rooms. The final bedroom, the largest of the four and on the first floor, was for the parents.

One of the two upstairs bathrooms was at the end of the hallway, and the other was directly off the master bedroom, which was where Sherry and Mary staked their claim. Closet space was at a premium.

While the children began to settle into their rooms, Bob, Katrina, and the movers finished unloading. When the truck had gone, all the children stayed in their rooms to finish settling in or to just relax after a long day of travel then moving in. That left Bob and Katrina alone to talk.

They discussed the abortion and the move, wondering if they had done all the right things. Katrina's parents had not been so forgiving of her when she got pregnant out of wedlock.

"Are we just telling her it is okay to have sex, that we'll fix it for her every time?" Katrina asked. "And are we giving that same message to Mary and Kim?"

Bob tried to reassure his wife. "I think it scared her enough to make her more careful who she goes out with from now on," he said. It was a weak attempt, and he knew it.

"That's hardly the point, being more selective with her dates," Katrina argued. "And it's not just Sherry I'm worried about."

She looked around to make sure none of the children were within earshot, then she lowered her voice for good measure. "Mary and Kim may already be thinking it's okay to have sex since their sister got away with it," she said.

Bob knew she was right but struggled with just how to approach it.

"I know what you mean," he said. "But we thought we were sending the right message to Sherry, and look what happened."

He thought back on the last several years and their approach with the children.

"Maybe we should have been more forceful in the way we talked to Sherry about it," he said.

The Dykes had also discussed sex with Terry, but being a boy, they weren't as concerned. While there would be consequences if he got a girl pregnant, they were viewed, not just by Bob and Katrina but also by society in general, minimal for boys. Perhaps because they would not be the ones carrying the child to birth. It was a bit of a sexist notion and a throwback to earlier times, but it prevailed nevertheless.

Bob and Katrina had not kept from the children, even Kim, the youngest, the fact that Terry was conceived before they were married. They believed in being open and honest with their children. It was their belief the kids should hear life matters, even those unpleasant or embarrassing, from them rather than others.

"Maybe, but now we have to consider whether we should take a different approach," Katrina said. "What we did before didn't work, so we need to do things differently."

"That's true," Bob answered. "But she told us she didn't want to hear any more about it. She wants to put it behind her and move forward."

"But that does not keep us from changing the way we talk to Mary, Ralph, and Kim," Katrina said. "And maybe we should even talk to Terry, since he's out there in the world now."

She knew the reputation of sailors, with a girl in every port and the like. Bob was also mindful of it. But that was a discussion for another time.

Bob let his wife's suggestion sink in a bit. He knew she was right but was having trouble visualizing just how to alter their approach with the younger children, let alone with Terry.

"You're right," he finally said. "But I think we need to make changes gradually."

Katrina agreed. But she had regrets about her own life that she did not want her daughter—or any of her children—to have to face. She had become pregnant with Terry when she was sixteen and gave birth just before her seventeenth birthday. While she and Bob took their parental responsibilities seriously and worked through their remaining years in high school to raise him, they did not marry until they had both graduated. Not long thereafter, Katrina discovered she was pregnant again. She had dreams of a career in the medical field and began taking classes at a small community college seventy-five miles from their small Wyoming home town. But it didn't take long to realize that the long commute took a toll on her academics and her young family. So she had to put her dream on hold.

Even prior to that experience, being parents and continuing their education did not leave much time for the usual high school social life most students have. While their friends were going to games, dances, and other activities, they were busy diapering, feeding, and caring for an infant in between their studies. Both their parents were insistent they finish high school, as well as be parents to the child. Abortion, for them, was never an option.

Both had planned to attend college, although Bob was still uncertain about an end goal, and were exploring how to do that with a child when Katrina got pregnant again shortly before the end of her senior year. Bob got a job in the local mill, and Katrina made her aborted attempt at college.

Through the years, Katrina tried to restart her college education, taking one or two classes per semester, including some introductory medical courses. But as the family got bigger with each additional child, it became harder. Finally, a few years before the move to Washington, she stopped taking classes and concentrated on being a working mother.

Bob had worked his way up at the mill, working at and learning every specific task on site. Eventually, he was promoted to yard foreman. While the work was good and paid well, Bob always wondered what would have happened had he and Katrina been able to pursue their plans for a college education.

Yes, there were regrets, for both of them, about the things they had given up. Regardless, they were happy with each other and happy with their family.

Chapter 2

Jim and Helen Baxter and their daughter, Karen, were nice people. As the Dykes' next-door neighbors, they introduced themselves the day after the move in and offered to help them in any way they could. Bob and Katrina readily accepted their friendship, and the two families began to work together to get the Dykes settled in and acclimated to Carson and the surrounding communities.

Karen was Sherry's age, and they got along very well. Both were attractive young women. Sherry was tall for a woman, standing just two inches short of six feet. She had her parents to thank for her height. Bob and Katrina were a perfectly matched six feet. Sherry also got her mother's auburn hair, and she grew it long, now to the middle of her back. Like her mother, Sherry was slim but curvy.

On the other hand, Karen stood five feet, two inches tall with a slim build. She wore her brunette hair short, just touching her shoulders.

Jim worked at the same mill where Bob would start in a few days. Helen was a stay-at-home mother, but she did some sewing, babysitting, and light housework from time to time to bring in extra money to the family.

The Dykes were dinner guests of the Baxters on their second day in Carson. After dinner, the adults sat around the Baxters' living room fireplace and got acquainted while the boys went outside to play. Sherry, Mary, and Kim went upstairs to spend time with Karen.

Sherry had made a friend in her new town already. She was beginning to feel like it was home.

The Dyke girls sat in rapt attention as Karen described Carson. They found there was no high school in town, so Sherry and Mary would attend in nearby Stevenson, as would Ralph for junior high school. Kim, on the other hand, would attend the elementary school in Carson.

Karen interrupted her dissertation on Carson at one point to ask Sherry if she had a boyfriend in her former hometown in Wyoming. That brought memories of Ted rushing into Sherry's mind. He was the father of the unborn baby.

Sherry had not had any steady boyfriends in Wyoming. She dated several boys at different times since entering high school. Ted had been the last of those. She didn't really have any strong feelings for him; he was just another date. None had lit any sparks for her.

But Ted Brennen, who was two years older than Sherry, was more aggressive sexually than any of the other boys she had dated. In their two-month relationship, he continually made advances toward her.

Sherry was no prude and had participated in heavy petting with more than one of her previous dates. But she stopped short of intercourse. But Ted was more insistent than the others.

One evening following a school dance, Ted drove his 1966 Ford Mustang with Sherry in the passenger seat to a secluded spot just outside of town. The couple began to kiss, leading to some fondling. After a short time, Ted, an athletic six-foot-two-inch man with a temper, pushed for more.

"It's time for us to get down to it," he said.

Sherry knew what he meant, and she was not ready to go that far. But he wasn't going to take no for an answer.

"We've been going out for two months," he told her. "It's time for us to move to the next level."

"What do you mean by 'next level'?" Sherry asked, knowing exactly what he meant but stalling for time.

"We need to have sex," Ted said. "I'm tired of this playing around."

"But I'm not ready," Sherry told him.

"You damned well better be ready," he said, moving in closer to her and reaching for her pants to unfasten them. "Otherwise, you're just a big prick teaser."

Ted's demeanor became physically aggressive. He had Sherry pinned against the passenger side door. She put her hands over the button on her jeans as he fumbled with it, but her move made him angry. He reached up and slapped her hard across the face.

"We're going to do this," he snarled at her. "I'm sick of being teased."

Due to a mixture of guilt, believing his assertion that she had teased him with an unspoken promise of sex, and fear from the increasing aggressive behavior from him, she moved her hands away and allowed him to unfasten her pants and pull them down, followed by her panties.

Ted reached down and pulled down his own pants and underwear. He pulled her down so she was lying across the two bucket seats, with her butt on the center console. Ted opened the driver's door and stretched his legs out as he sprawled on top of Sherry. He placed her right leg over the steering column and her left foot propped behind the headrest.

He then put his hard cock onto her crotch and rubbed it up and down along her vaginal lips until he felt them open slightly. He pushed himself inside her, but not very far. Having never had intercourse before and in the fear of the moment, Sherry was not open to him. But he thrusted as hard as he could a few times until her hymen popped, and then he went deep inside her. He continued thrusting until he climaxed with a satisfying sigh.

Sherry was not satisfied at all. She was in pain, and she felt warm liquid between her legs. She first thought it was his ejaculate. But she learned differently as he started to get up and pull up his pants.

"You bitch!" he yelled. "You got blood on my car."

He grabbed a towel from the back seat and wiped the center console as she hurriedly pulled on her panties and jeans. She later, from the preliminary examination before the abortion, learned that his violent thrusting had torn some tissue inside her.

In the days and weeks following the incident, he tried to see her again, but she steadfastly refused. A month later, she discovered she was pregnant, which set in motion the events that took her and her family to Carson.

The memory of it all made Sherry a little sick to her stomach as she sat in Karen's room with her younger siblings. But she did her best to hide it.

Sherry did tell Karen about Ted, but she left out the pregnancy and the event that produced it. She did not want anyone in her new hometown to know that part of her past. She did explain they had not been going steady, that there really had been no steady for her yet.

"Did you love him?" Karen asked.

Although it shouldn't have, the question surprised Sherry. She paused a few seconds before answering.

"No, not really," she said.

"Was he good-looking?" Karen was curious.

Sherry did not answer. Talking about Ted, even in an abstract way, just kept bringing back all the bad memories she was fighting to forget. Her discomfort finally showed.

"What's wrong?" Karen asked. "Hey, if you don't want to talk about it, we don't have to."

"I don't want to, thanks," Sherry said. The relief in her voice was louder than an explosion.

Both to learn more about the town and to see her new friend again, Sherry asked Karen the following day to show her around. While she and Mary had seen mostly everything there was to see their first day, Karen helped provide a little context.

"There's not much here for stores," Karen told her. "This is a logging town, so most of the businesses are mechanics, machine shops, and things like that."

There were a few more shops in Stevenson and Cascade Locks across the river and in White Salmon on the Washington side and Hood River on the Oregon side. But those were longer drives.

"We should plan a day trip to Vancouver or Portland to do some real shopping," Karen said.

Sherry would look forward to that.

During the walking tour, they went into the fabric shops Sherry and Mary had discovered. It had a good selection of fabrics, but limited clothing. They also went into both the general stores on Wind River Highway. In the second one, there were only a few shoppers milling about and only two employees—an adult man at the front counter and a boy about Sherry's age working in the rear of the store. The boy caught sight of the girls and went to the front of the store as they left. He watched as they walked up the street.

There was also a restaurant and a bar along their walk. They visited each one briefly, including poking their heads in the front door of the bar. At about 1:00 p.m., it already had several customers. That fact struck Sherry that this town and her previous home were very much alike.

The girls talked about a wide variety of things. Karen kept her promise not to ask about Ted anymore. But it did not stop her curiosity from growing by leaps and bounds.

When they returned to the house, Katrina asked Sherry to help her with some unpacking that had not been completed the day before. Karen took the opportunity to invite Mary alone to her house.

"What is it with Sherry?" she asked once they were in her room. "Did this guy Ted do something to her?"

Mary was a little surprised and irritated at the questions. She heard Karen make the promise the day before. She believed it was a promise not to talk about it at all, not just avoid talking to Sherry about it.

"No," was her only response, hoping that would end the inquiry. But she misjudged Karen's tenacity.

"Then why does she hate to talk about him?" Karen was persistent.

"I don't know," Mary responded, again hoping it would end Karen's questions on that subject. It was in vain.

"He must have done something," she went on. "Did he beat her, get her pregnant, what?"

When the word *pregnant* came out of Karen's mouth, Mary reacted with a worried look then realized Karen had seen it. Mary turned her face away, hoping against hope that Karen did not pick up on her apprehension.

"He beat her," Karen said. Mary shook her head.

"He got her pregnant then," Karen offered.

"No!" the answer came back in an instant and much too forceful.

"He did, didn't he?" Karen said with satisfaction. "But what happened to the baby?"

Mary felt trapped. Obviously, Karen knew she had hit on the right answer. Continued denials on Mary's part would only increase her inquisitiveness. If she refused to talk about it, she feared the same result. But she had promised her sister she would not discuss it with anyone, especially in their new surroundings.

In that awkward moment, she weighed all the options. She believed, as her parents had always told their children, the truth was the best route. Mary believed she could minimize the damage.

"All right, yes, he did get her pregnant," Mary almost spit it out, like rejecting sour milk. "But you can't talk about this with anyone, not even Sherry."

Karen nodded, but Mary knew that little tidbit of information was not going to satisfy her curiosity.

"She had an abortion," Mary said hesitantly. "She did not want to raise a baby alone."

It was not the whole truth but all she was willing to offer.

"But what about the guy, what about Ted?" Karen asked, seeming to get angry. "He wasn't willing to help?"

Mary shook her head.

"What did his parents think about that?" Karen asked.

"They didn't know. Even Ted didn't know about the baby," Mary explained, leaving out the part that he later found out and made their lives miserable.

"So how did Sherry know he didn't want to help with the baby?" Karen asked.

"One time he had told her that he didn't want to have any kids," Mary said, hoping the white lie would pass muster. Because the questions just kept coming, she was regretting her decision to talk about it. Karen kept pressing.

Finally, Mary had had enough.

"I've said way more than I should have," she said, getting up from the floor next to the bed where they had been sitting. "It's time for me to go."

"Wait," Karen said, struggling to get up before Mary could leave the room. "I didn't mean to make you angry."

"I'm not angry, just worried," Mary said.

"Worried about what?" Karen asked.

"I promised Sherry I would never tell anyone," Mary said. "She'll kill me if she finds out I told you."

Karen reached out and put her hand on Mary's shoulder.

"I'll keep your secret," she assured her. "I won't tell anyone."

Mary gave a weak smile, already certain that her sister's secret would get out, and it would be all her fault. She left Karen's house more worried than she had ever been. She loved Sherry and cherished their closeness. If the secret of the pregnancy and abortion got out in their new hometown, their bond would be forever broken if Sherry discovered her sister had shared the secret with anyone.

The phone on Karen's desk jingled on its cradle.

"Hello," she said.

"Karen? This is Barry," the voice on the other end said. "Who was that chick with you in the store today?"

"That was Sherry Dyke. She moved in next door to us yesterday," Karen explained. "Why?"

"I want to meet her."

"Oh, really?" Karen said teasingly. "When would you like to meet her?"

"Whenever."

"Okay. Go to the pool in Stevenson tomorrow at noon," Karen instructed. "We'll be there."

"Okay, I'll see you tomorrow then," Barry said.

"Tomorrow," Karen answered and hung up.

She couldn't wait to tell Sherry about it. Karen's excitement knew no bounds, but Sherry was less excited.

"I don't know," she told Karen. "I just don't want to get involved too quickly."

"But why?" Karen whined. "Barry is nice, and I think he likes you."

"But that's just it. He might want to get serious, and I don't want to."

"It still wouldn't hurt to meet him," Karen said. "Just tell him you don't want to get serious, and I'm sure he'll understand."

"But what if he doesn't?" Sherry asked. "I don't want to hurt him." With the memories of Ted resurfacing, Sherry was more worried about getting hurt herself, and not just emotionally.

"Don't worry. You won't," Karen assured her. "Just go and meet him, please."

"All right, but that's all," Sherry said. "No dates or anything like that."

"Agreed," Karen said excitedly. "I'll come and get you at eleven o'clock, okay?"

The next morning, as she was getting ready to go to Stevenson, Sherry still wasn't sure she had made the right decision in agreeing to meet Barry. She had decided she didn't want to get serious with any guy again. Her experience with Ted put it in her mind that she could not trust any other male who was not family. She wasn't even interested in having male friends.

But on the other hand, Sherry had been a very friendly, outgoing, and trusting person before she got involved with Ted. She liked that version of her personality, and there were times when she wished to be that person again.

There was a very intense conflict within Sherry Dyke. Self-preservation was driving her to be someone she was not—and did not like. The memories of herself before Ted were strong. But so far, not strong enough to erase the bad memories of her involvement with him and its aftermath.

But the whole idea of uprooting her entire family for this move to Washington was for a fresh start. If that were to come to pass, she would have to get past her fears and put some effort into that fresh start. Sherry knew that she could not just sit back and wait for good things to happen. She had to be a part of making them happen. That also meant opening herself up to emotional risk.

For that reason alone, she decided she had to give this guy a chance to at least meet her, since that was what he wanted. Maybe he was nice, like Karen had said. She conceded that she could become friends with him. *But only friends,* she reminded herself as she slipped into her two-piece flowered bikini.

As she looked at herself in the full-length mirror, some doubt crept into her mind. The swimwear revealed a lot of bare skin. The top covered her entire breasts, but it formed a shallow *V* in the middle where it connected between them. It revealed about two inches of cleavage. It reminded her of the behind-the-back whispering from the older adults in Wyoming that had filtered back to her.

"Girls who dress like that are just advertising themselves for sex."

"That's just trampish."

"I wouldn't be caught dead in something like that."

Sherry's attire had not been outrageous, but it was not prudish either. She wore tight-fitting shirts, but not form-fitting; some of her shirts were open at the top of the chest, showing only a hint of cleavage, if any, although not allowed at school. She also wore miniskirts and hot pants, which were the trend.

Sherry quickly went to her mother's room and found her one-piece swimsuit. Her mother was slightly taller and slightly more full-figured than Sherry. Without taking off the bikini, she slipped into her mother's black suit with the flowered fringe on top and went back into her room to look at the image in the mirror.

The suit fit well, but a bit loose. The design had her chest covered, showing no cleavage whatsoever, with straps over the shoulders. Sherry was satisfied and decided to wear her mother's swimsuit instead. After stripping off both suits and putting her mother's back on, she put on a pair of shorts and loose-fitting, thin blouse on over the suit.

When Karen came to pick her up, Sherry wasn't quite ready. She had Karen help her get the rest of her things together—towel, sunblock, and some other items. When it was all together and Sherry was finally ready to go, Karen asked her if she was excited about going to meet Barry.

"What's there to be excited about?" she asked as she went out the front door.

Inwardly, Sherry had a mix of emotions over this outing. There was excitement over exploring the area and even meeting someone new, hopefully more than one new person. But there was also anxiety about meeting a boy who wanted to meet her based only on a quick glimpse in a store.

Sherry was attractive enough to turn boys' heads. Her long auburn hair hung to the middle of her back, and when she curled it, there was a Farrah Fawcett look to her. While humble in many ways, Sherry knew boys found her attractive. But she never let it get to her head and certainly not after the incident with Ted as she was always trying to downplay her looks, as her indecision about swimwear showed.

Sherry also felt a certain amount of fear. She was afraid of how people in her new communities—as Carson and Stevenson were somewhat codependent—would perceive her.

The drive to Stevenson down State Route 14, or the Lewis and Clark Highway as it was sometimes called, was a quiet one. Sherry was still amazed at the lovely scenery that made up the entire area. She couldn't get over the feeling that she was in a storybook setting. It was just too beautiful to be true.

On both sides of the roadway, a variety of tall broadleaf trees mixed with Ponderosa pine were gathered like a crowd in an outdoor concert. On their left, the trees were thick enough to obscure the Columbia River, about a mile across to the Oregon side. But when they got to the edge of Stevenson itself, the roadway was nearly at the river's edge, and a beautiful panorama opened up to her view.

To the west, she could see the wide expanse of the river and the sharp curve of land on the Washington side where the river narrowed to about one-quarter of its width. She could not see it yet from her vantage point, but she knew the Bridge of the Gods spanned the Columbia River at its narrowest point in the area and connected State Route 14 with Interstate 80 in Oregon.

Scientists believed more than one thousand years ago, a giant landslide on the north side of the river at the location of the modern bridge created a natural dam that created an inland sea that stretched as far east as the state of Idaho. Eventually, erosion cut a hole in the bottom of the barrier, creating a natural bridge across the river. That bridge eventually collapsed, creating the Cascade Rapids.

Construction on the modern steel truss cantilever bridge started in 1920, and it opened for traffic in 1926.

Sherry could not wait to explore more of the area.

Chapter 3

Sherry loved to swim. However, the opportunity to do so was limited in her former hometown in Wyoming.

The winter weather made outdoor swimming impossible, except during June, July, and August. Even then, there were limitations. The only public pool in town was at a motel, and the hours allowed for townspeople to use it were short. In addition, Wyoming summers could be unpredictable. During her life there, Sherry had seen, although rare in the summer months, snowfall during every month of the year.

There would have been limits to swimming in their new home had it not been for the indoor pool in Stevenson, built in 1957. Gorge winters could be as cold as Wyoming's, and while there was little or no snow at the edges of the Gorge, during the summer months, temperatures could get quite chilly when the wind howled up and down the Gorge. Even during calm days, the river itself kept temperatures down with all that moisture.

So Sherry was pleased not only to find out there was a public pool nearby but that it was indoors. That meant swimming excursions year-round.

When she and Karen arrived at the facility, she wasted no time getting in the pool. She relaxed in the warm water, alternating between just floating near the side and swimming short distances, using different styles. So comfortable was the atmosphere that she forgot the reason she had let Karen talk her into coming.

During one of Sherry's floating sessions, Karen swam to her and pointed to the edge of the pool. There, looking out across the water stood a boy about six feet tall. His bright blond hair and muscular build made him stand out among the mostly preadolescents coming and going on the pool deck. From where she was, Sherry could see that his eyes were the brightest blue she had ever seen.

Karen told her to follow, and she started across the pool toward the boy. Sherry hesitated. She was suddenly unsure if this was a wise thing to do at this stage in her time in the new environment. Karen stopped midway across the pool and motioned for her to come on. Feeling a bit put on the spot, she nearly climbed out of the pool and would have headed straight for the dressing room. But after some thought, she decided it wouldn't hurt, so she followed Karen across the pool to where the boy stood. He saw them coming toward him, and he went to the side of the pool.

"Hi, Barry, this is Sherry Dyke," Karen said, motioning to each in turn. "Sherry, this is Barry Walker," Karen said as the two girls got to the pool's edge.

"Hi," was Barry's shy answer.

"I heard you wanted to meet me," Sherry said, trying to take the initiative.

"Yeah, I did," Barry said. "I saw you at the store, and I just wanted to meet you."

"I am very flattered," she said, now feeling a little blush come to her cheeks.

"Well, when you two are done, how about going downtown and I'll buy you a soda or something?" Barry offered.

The two girls looked at each other. Giving agreeable looks, they accepted his offer.

They sat in a booth at the Dairy Queen, each with a drink in front of them and a large container of french fries between them. The trio talked almost nonstop. Both Barry and Sherry did not say much until prodded by Karen, who acted like a moderator at a political debate.

Barry's and Sherry's reluctance to talk came from different motivations. Barry was naturally shy and not a conversation starter. He could be involved in personal interaction, but he rarely got the ball rolling, instead waiting for others to start talking, and he would chip in from time to time.

Sherry picked up on that trait and, on one hand, was kind of attracted by it but, on the other hand, wished he would talk more—partly so she didn't have to.

Sherry's input to the conversation was not as aggressive because she was being cautious. She did not want to talk about what happened in Wyoming. But she knew that when people are relaxed in their conversations, they tended to be more open with things that were best left unsaid.

For her part, Karen was a good moderator. Whenever the conversation lagged, she was quick to prod each to talk about a certain aspect of their life.

Sherry learned that Barry had lived in Stevenson most of his life. Wanting a simpler life and environment for their family, his parents moved to the Gorge from the Portland metro area in Oregon before he was ten years old. Sherry also learned that Barry was the youngest of three children in the family.

Barry dabbled in every sport offered at Stevenson High School. Basketball was his favorite, but it was only in his junior year that he got to see some playing time on the varsity team. Like his father and older brother, he was into hunting and fishing. His interest was not as intense as his father or brother, but he had been on enough trips with them to pick up quick a few outdoor and survival skills.

That appealed to Sherry on a certain level. While none of her immediate family were avid hunters or fishermen, they all enjoyed being in nature, so camping trips were numerous.

One other thing Sherry learned that day was that the more Barry talked about himself, although reluctantly, the more she wanted to hear. Sherry came to the realization that she was becoming attracted to this boy.

That sent a shiver of fright down her spine. But at the same time, she couldn't help but want to explore that attraction.

"Will I see you again?" Barry asked Sherry when she and Karen were ready to go back to Carson.

"Probably," she said, a bit puzzled.

She remained puzzled when she got home. What did he mean when he asked her if he would see her again? she thought. Was he hung up on her? She didn't want to think about it, but it kept creeping into her mind.

Sherry did see Barry Walker again. As the summer went on, she and Barry got together regularly. After a few times, she began to feel an attraction to him. Soon, they were almost never apart. Many times, she would talk Karen into taking her to Stevenson. Other times, Barry would drive his blue 1970 Grand Prix to Carson to see her.

At first, Sherry was uncertain about increased contact with Barry. But as time went on, she began to put the unpleasant memories of Ted, the abortion, and the judgment and harassment of her former hometown behind her. Sherry felt her caution begin to ease.

Karen was happy. She had introduced them, and now it appeared the two were hitting it off. She was happy for her new friend.

Sherry confided in Karen during a trip to the Portland area for some shopping and sightseeing that she thought she might be falling in love.

The drive to Oregon's largest city helped whittle down Sherry's wall of caution in talking about her Wyoming experience. Karen did the driving since she was more familiar with the area. Sherry had the time, between snatches of conversation, to watch as they crossed the Bridge of the Gods and connected with Interstate 80 heading west.

She marveled at how the Columbia River narrowed so quickly where the bridge spanned the water, created by the Table Mountain landslide hundreds of years ago. The high cliffs on the Oregon side of the river were covered with trees, creating a dark forest-green carpet for miles. The color scheme was much the same on the Washington side, but the mountains rose up more gradually.

Karen pushed her 1957 Chevy Bel Air up to speed on the freeway, and a few minutes later, Sherry caught a glimpse through the trees to her right of the Bonneville Dam complex. Situated in a large "bowl" as the river suddenly widened, the three giant structures were in between three islands inside the river bowl. Between the southernmost island and the riverbank were locks to allow water vessels to go past the dam.

"So it looks like you and Barry are getting along quite well," Sherry heard Karen say.

She felt her cheeks get warm and knew they were red from the rush of blood at the unexpected question. She kept her head turned to the right, looking out the car window at the trees and river beyond rushing by, in hopes Karen did not see her blushing.

"Yeah, we are," she answered.

"Is that all, just getting along?" Karen asked, shifting her eyes to Sherry briefly to see if there was any reaction. In that instant, before turning back to the roadway, she saw Sherry's left check go from rouge red to its normal skin color.

"That's all," Sherry responded and turned to look at her friend. "That's all I want right now."

"Do you think you might want more with him someday?" Karen asked.

Sherry thought about it for a moment. Sure, she thought, the answer was yes. But there was also a part of her that was still afraid of getting into a relationship with a boy. But she wasn't sure she wanted to share that with anyone, including Karen, who had become her closest friend.

"Anything is possible," Sherry finally said. "But I'm not looking for anything more."

The two girls were silent for a couple of miles.

"I do have some feelings for Barry," Sherry suddenly said, surprising even herself. "But at this point, I don't really know what to make of them."

"That's okay," Karen said. "I'm not trying to push you into something."

"I know," Sherry answered.

Again, a few miles of silence. Then Sherry spoke again. "Do you think I am being unfair to Barry?"

Karen vigorously shook her head.

"No, I don't think you're being unfair," Karen said. "As long as you really are serious about not wanting anything besides his friendship."

She paused for a moment, and when Sherry did not respond, she went on.

"If you do love him, even a little bit, you do need to talk to him about it," she said.

"What would I say to him?" Sherry asked after a short pause.

"You need to be honest," Karen said.

Sherry swallowed a lump in her throat.

"What if what I tell him turns him away?" she asked. "I really don't want that to happen, you know, in case my feelings turn into something else."

This time, it was Karen's turn to take a moment to gather her thoughts. She did not know Barry real well, only as casual acquaintances. She really had no idea how he might react because she could tell that he was certainly smitten with Sherry. She believed in that moment that it could go either way.

"I can't tell you how he would take it if you just wanted to be his friend," Karen said, wanting to be honest with her friend. "I believe he feels very strongly for you. So it could be a big disappointment."

She glanced at Sherry to gauge her reaction. She saw fright in her expression as she stared straight ahead.

"You owe it to him to be honest, even if all you want from him is friendship," Karen said.

Sherry knew her friend was right.

It was three days after the Portland trip with Karen that Sherry talked to Barry about their relationship. It took her that long to build up the courage to do so and to determine just what she would say.

Barry had a day off, so he offered to take her to Multnomah Falls. The popular spot on the Oregon side of the river features a waterfall fed by underground springs from Larch Mountain. It is actually two sets of falls. The main set drops 542 feet into a small pool at the base then flows over a second set, dropping 59 feet. Visitors access both falls through a trail that also crosses Benson Bridge, just above the lower falls.

Sherry remembered the falls from her previous visit and wanted to see the site again as quickly as possible after they settled into their new home.

They were at the National Scenic Area in a short time. But Sherry had said nothing on the drive. She didn't want Barry distracted from driving, plus she wanted his full attention.

On the walk from the parking lot through the tunnel under the railroad tracks and across the scenic highway, they chitchatted about Sherry's memories of the falls from years before. Barry was interested in what she had to say. He wanted to know all he could about this girl who had so captured his attention, and possibly even his heart. So except for a few questions here and there, he was content to listen to her.

They decided to skip the ornate lodge adjacent to the highway for now. The Cascadian-style brick-and-lumber building housed a restaurant, gift shop, snack shop, and interpretive center.

The pair hiked up the trail, over the arched stone Benson Bridge, and to the observation platform at the base of the main falls. Despite the warm weather on this summer morning, the mist from the falls and the platform in full shadow made Sherry shiver. She pulled on the windbreaker she had brought along for protection against possible wind in the Gorge.

They stood in silence for a few moments.

Sherry had contemplated beginning her talk with Barry during their trek to the upper falls. But as they passed by the lower falls, the roar of the water made it difficult to hear, and the same was true at the upper falls. So she decided to wait.

In the meantime, she stood in awe at the cascading water falling more than five hundred feet straight down, mostly through the air instead of against the cliff. She marveled at the power the falling water had behind it by the time it splashed into the pool at the base. She could tell the pool was deep, providing testimony to the erosion the water exerted as it pounded into the ground over the years.

They were silent again as they descended back to the lodge. Sherry took in the sight of the river, beginning to widen again at this point. Across the river, she saw the sheer rock cliffs of Cape Horn,

State Route 14 up high on the cliff jutting out at one point on stone pillars, and the railway at the base of the cliff.

She drank in the sights with a sense of awe and wonder. The marvel of their creation, both by nature and man, was something she could not comprehend, but she wanted to.

They had lunch at the lodge restaurant, and after they had placed their orders, Sherry decided the time had come. She had run through her mind all morning what she planned to say to him. It was very clear in her mind, so it was best to get it said now before the words found their way out of her mind.

"Barry, there is something I want to talk to you about," she said cautiously. He picked up on the hesitation in her voice.

"Okay, I am ready and willing to listen," he answered, trying to put some levity in his tone to try and put her at ease. He could tell it helped a little.

"You have been very kind and friendly to me," she began, paused for a second or two, then went on. "I want you to know that I appreciate that very much."

She paused again, and Barry moved forward in his seat, dipped his head a little, and tilted it to one side and looked at her with his upturned eyes.

"But...," he said, still trying to provide a lighter side to what sounded like the beginning of a very serious conversation.

Sherry felt her heart seem to skip a beat, and the breath caught in her throat. The last thing she wanted to do was alienate this boy. She quickly regained her composure, but Barry had noticed the panic in her eyes.

"But you are worried I want to get serious or, worse, just want your body," Barry said before Sherry could speak. Now Sherry was frantically searching for the well-prepared speech that suddenly seemed to have disappeared.

"Well, yes, something like that," she finally stammered.

Barry sat back in his seat, a broad smile on his face briefly. He then turned serious.

"Sherry, you and I have known each other less than two weeks," he said. "That's hardly enough time to get to know each other."

Sherry started to speak, but he held up his right hand with one finger in the air.

"And I don't want to just get into your pants," he said.

At that moment, the waitress brought his pastrami sandwich and her tuna melt. The server, a woman in her thirties, looked at each of them in turn, hoping to hear more of the conversation.

"Thank you," Barry said politely, but a little dismissively. The waitress walked away disappointed. Barry turned back to Sherry. "I am not against getting serious," he told her. "But I would want to get to know you well before that happened. I would want to make sure we are compatible."

He could see the relief in her face.

"And I suspect you believe the same," he added.

She nodded and took a small bite of her sandwich.

"As for the other thing, I'm not saying I don't want to get into your pants," he said with a twinkle in his eye. "But that's only something I would try with someone I decided I wanted to be serious with…and who wanted to be serious with me."

Sherry reached her hand across the table, palm up, and Barry took hold of it. Sherry squeezed his hand gently.

"Thank you," she said.

Chapter 4

The remainder of the summer passed quickly.

The Dykes settled into their new home and began to build the same kind of atmosphere they had in their former home in Wyoming. Bob was busy at the mill from early morning to early evening, but he still found time to socialize during his off-hours and on weekends. But he made sure to chisel out enough time to spend with the family.

Katrina was able to get a job fairly quickly as a waitress and cook at a small diner adjacent to State Route 14, where it intersected with Wind River Highway that ran south down the western edge of Carson. The diner was small, with enough room only for the kitchen, a counter with six stools, and two booths. But the money she made there was enough to supplement Bob's income.

The Baxters were a large help in getting the Dyke parents integrated into the community. They hosted dinners at their home and included the Dykes and various of their Carson friends so they could all get acquainted. They all took a liking to the entire Dyke family.

Sherry and her younger siblings also made new friends, partly by introductions from the Baxters' dinner guests and partly from their own exploration of the community.

Since she was fourteen, Sherry had summer jobs to allow her to earn her own spending money, even through the previous summer before leaving Wyoming. But this summer, her parents discouraged that. They wanted her to concentrate on exploring college opportunities following her final year in high school. They wanted her to make sure college was in her future, since they had both missed out on the opportunity.

They expected to follow the same plan after each of their children completed their junior years.

They had done the same with Terry, and he planned to attend college after his initial hitch in the Navy ended, unless he decided to make it a career.

With no job for the summer, she had plenty of time to make friends while she waited for Barry to finish with his summer job. In this, she had plenty of help from Karen Baxter, who introduced her to nearly all the Stevenson High School students who lived in Carson and a large number from Stevenson on their frequent trips downriver to that town for swimming and other activities.

As for her and Barry, they spent a great deal of time together when he was not working. At first, they stuck to their plan agreed upon in the Multnomah Falls Lodge restaurant that they would get to know each other quite well before deciding whether to plunge into a romantic relationship.

What they learned of each other led to deeper feelings for each.

When they were alone together, their conversations became easier, since they both had to contribute more heavily. While Sherry was open with talk about her personality, she was more cautious about revealing too much of her past. She shared that she had been involved in a number of activities at her former school, including the pep club, chorus, drama club, and in her last year there, the yearbook staff.

Barry could tell she was very guarded, especially when he asked if there had been a boyfriend she left behind.

"No," she answered too quickly and forcefully. "I mean, I did date a little, but there was no one steady," she said sheepishly after seeing his surprised look.

"It's okay. I was just wondering," he said.

Sherry was now fully embarrassed. She had been caught off guard and said the first thing that came to her panicked mind. She was so afraid that as their conversation became more casual, she would let her guard down and say something about Ted, and then she would have to explain the whole story to Barry.

It wasn't that she planned to keep the truth from him if they did end up in a serious relationship. She just wanted to wait until that happened, if it, in fact, did. There was also a part of her that feared that if Barry knew about her past regarding the pregnancy and abortion, it would turn him off and that would ruin any chance of a serious relationship.

And the more she got to know Barry, she began to want that to happen.

She found Barry to be easygoing, sensitive, and gentle. He treated her with respect and even a bit of reverence. They seemed to have many things in common and rarely disagreed, including in their outlook for life. Those times when they found themselves on opposite sides of something, he was not argumentative. She found him to be a good listener.

It was still the same when school started in September. They were both seniors and were seen together almost constantly.

Sherry's parents were worried at first. But they soon saw she had to live her own life, so they didn't interfere. Later on, they saw there was no need to worry. The more Sherry and Barry were together, the more their bond grew, and by Christmas, there was nothing that would separate them.

It was Sherry who upped the ante on their relationship.

She and Barry took a drive to Portland just for a chance to get out of their Gorge homes for some time away from family and friends. Ever since school started, they had been busy with activities and, especially during the holidays, family get-togethers that they had nearly no time to just be alone together.

Sherry had joined the pep club. Barry had encouraged her to try and get on the cheerleading squad, but tryouts had been conducted and the squad chosen just as the last school year was ending. Sherry also got on the yearbook staff.

Barry was involved in football to start the year. He was an average athlete and did not get into the starting lineup for the Bulldogs but was a good utility player. Coaches subbed him into games to spell other players for a few plays. As a running back and receiver, he had carried and caught the ball a few times, and as a defensive back, he did have a few tackles and recovered a fumble.

In October, he went with his father and brother on hunting trips. As he was not as into it as they were, he was a half-hearted participant, enjoying instead the opportunity to spend time in the backwoods north of Carson.

When football season was over, he transitioned into basketball, his favorite of the school's sports. Despite it being his favorite, he did not crack the starting lineup, but he did play often as the team's first substitute when needed.

To be near Sherry more, he also joined the yearbook staff and learned photography and darkroom skills on the fly.

Sherry and Barry reminisced about the school year and their friendship so far during their trip to Portland. The last stop was the Jantzen Beach Center on Hayden Island in Portland near the Columbia River. The area had been an amusement park until 1970, and the shopping center opened in 1972.

Sherry vaguely remembered the amusement park from her previous trip to the Pacific Northwest. But the only reminder of that facility was the 1921-built C. W. Parker carousel now located inside the main center area.

After riding the carousel, Barry and Sherry sat and watched others enjoy the ride, mostly children, while their parents shopped at nearby stores. During a short break in their chitchat, Sherry made a bold move. She threw her arms around him, turned his face toward hers, and gave him a lasting first kiss.

As she pulled away, she could see he was surprised, but pleasantly so. He reached up and caressed her cheek with his hand.

"Does this mean what I think it means?" he asked.

Sherry flushed lightly. She knew the answer was yes, and she wanted so badly to not just say it but scream it so that it echoed through the center, drowning out the circus melodies of the carousel. But now she was suddenly afraid he would not feel the same. Sheepishly, she nodded.

The smile spreading across his face gave her the relief she was hoping for.

"I have been wanting to do that myself for some time," Barry said. "But I wasn't sure you felt the same."

They shared a laugh together and hugged tightly.

* * *

Sawmill work could be a dangerous occupation depending on a person's experience level and where in the mill they were assigned. For the most part, people worked in specific areas based on their particular skills and time in those areas. But there were times when someone in one area was needed to fill in at a spot when the person filling that role was out sick or had a doctor's appointment or a family emergency.

One day, just after the turn of the new year, Sam Trueblood found a note on his time card when he reported for work at the mill in Home Valley. Instead of operating the trim saw, he was to report to what was commonly called the double saw. His usual station was like a huge band saw that trimmed the rounded edges off logs to prepare them to be cut into boards. The double saw was the next station, designed to cut the trimmed logs, now resembling long boxes, into eight-foot lengths before they were rip cut into boards.

The double saw operator's position was standing in a round waist-high steel-sided pit. Conveyor belts on each side fed the square logs along until they hit a marker that designated eight feet from the mark to the fifteen-foot diameter circular saw that swung down to cut the logs.

The conveyors and saws were controlled manually by the operator using three buttons, a set on each side of the pit in direct alignment with the saws. Two were for the conveyor, one for forward and one for reverse. The other was for the saw. The pit was only slightly larger than a fifty-five-gallon drum, so the operator worked in a tight environment.

An experienced operator could move the double lines of logs along at a pretty good pace with hardly a hesitation, even if a conveyor or saw jammed because of debris from the logs. It was a matter of watching with peripheral vision to watch both markers and stop the conveyor at the right time then hitting the saw button for the cut.

Sam had operated the double saw a number of times. But since it was not his normal station, he was a bit slower than the regular operator. It slowed production, but it was something mill foremen had to accept from time to time. But the pressure to step it up was always there.

This particular day, Sam was keeping things moving at a pretty good pace. But after about two hours, the right-side conveyor jammed because of a large splinter that had split off the front end of a log as he hit the button to move it forward. About the size of a baseball bat, the splinter was jammed in pretty tight, so tight that reversing and moving the conveyor forward a couple of times did not clear it.

Sam had to clear it manually.

In a case like this, mill rules stated the operator should exit the pit and, standing on the small platform in front of it, putting him at a distance from the saw, pull the debris out. But because the splinter was within reach from the pit and, knowing the stated procedure would stop production all along the line for a few minutes, he believed he could clear it from within the pit.

He reached out and grabbed the end of the splinter that jutted out toward him. He pulled as hard as he could, but it did not budge. He pulled twice more with no success. He decided to try something else before exiting the pit.

Sam braced himself to pull the splinter then nudged the forward conveyor button with his hip. The conveyor lurched forward, and the splinter, caught in the belt teeth, jerked forward, yanking Sam's arms with it. The motion pulled him forward, so he couldn't hit the conveyor button again with his hip to stop it. It also made him release the splinter with his right hand, but his glove on the left hand was caught on a jutting, ragged knot. Sam braced his right hand on the pit rim and jerked his arm back, and his hand came away from the splinter.

But the sudden release threw him back and to the right, and his hip hit the saw button, sending it swinging down. In that split second, Sam knew his flailing right arm would come within the arch of the saw. But because of the speed of the saw, he felt no pain as it tore into his right wrist, slicing it neatly diagonally across the joint.

Several workers in the area saw Sam's efforts and his jerking body as the splinter and saw did its work. They shut down their equipment, one sounding the alarm that signaled for all machinery to come to a halt by way of the master switch in the shop foreman's platform, and rushed to the double saw station. They found Sam half crouching in the pit with his right arm flopped on the side and his left hanging at his side. Widening pools of blood were under each.

His coworkers quickly tied tourniquets above each wrist with their belts. They saw his right hand, still in its glove, was nearly severed, hanging on by only a few inches of skin, small muscles, and tendons. His left hand was missing the outer three fingers just past the knuckles in the hand itself. A worker found his glove lying on the small platform with the fingers still inside, with a long, thin tendon extending out about the length of his forearm.

* * *

Sherry was busy taking notes in Stephen Kawalski's US government class when there was a knock on the classroom door. The popular teacher interrupted his discussion of the Fourteenth Amendment to the US Constitution and opened the door. Even those in the front-row seats, three ahead of where Sherry sat, could not hear what was being whispered to Mr. Kawalski.

He turned a concerned look toward Bev Trueblood sitting three seats to Sherry's right.

"Bev, could you please go with Miss Planot to the office." It was not a request.

Bev slowly got up from her seat and took a step toward the door.

"Please take your things with you," Mr. Kawalski said apologetically.

She hesitated then gathered her books and purse and headed for the main office.

GORGE JUSTICE

Bev was a good student and certainly not a troublemaker. So Sherry was wondering why she would be called out of class to the main office. That was usually reserved for those who acted out. Trying to figure it out interfered with her concentration as Mr. Kawalski returned to his discussion. But the entire class could see even he was having trouble concentrating on the subject.

Ten minutes later, there was another knock at the door. When it was opened, Karen was standing just outside, and she whispered to the teacher, just like Miss Planot had. He turned his gaze to Sherry.

"Karen is in need of your help, Sherry," he said. "She has your pass to leave the school."

Sherry gathered her belongings and tried to stay calm. Why were she and Bev taken from the classroom? The two had been introduced by Karen and had become friends, but they were not close, not like Sherry and Karen. Sherry knew little about Bev as they spent little time together.

The mystery was explained as they walked the hallway to the office.

"I need to take Bev to the hospital, and I need your help," Karen told her. "We need to stop in Carson and get her little brother."

Bev and Bruce were the Truebloods' only children. Bruce was a fifth grader at Carson Elementary School.

"What's happening?" Sherry asked.

"Bev's dad was hurt real bad at the mill," Karen answered. "His wife is on her way to the hospital, and she called the school to tell Bev. She wanted the kids to get there as fast as possible. Bev asked if I would take her."

"What happened to her dad?" Sherry asked, concerned not just for Sam but for her own father, knowing he worked at the same mill.

"I don't know the details," Karen said as they prepared to enter the office. "I just know it's bad."

After collecting Bev, who was still shaken, the girls climbed into Karen's Bel Air. Sherry sat in the back seat with Bev to try and comfort her as best she could. They stopped briefly in Carson to pick up a confused Bruce. He wasn't told why he needed to leave school.

Sherry beckoned him to sit in the back with her and his sister. He climbed in and started asking questions.

"What's going on?" he asked.

"Dad was hurt at the mill," Bev said, her voice breaking. "Mom wants us at the hospital."

"What happened to Dad?" he asked.

His sister started to speak, but the words caught in her throat.

"We don't really know what happened or how bad it is," Sherry told Bruce. "But I'll bet he'll be okay."

It was an empty promise, and Sherry knew it. But she wanted to be as optimistic as possible for the two siblings.

Both were silent the rest of the twenty-mile drive that Karen covered in just under twenty minutes.

Chapter 5

Sam Trueblood's injuries were severe.

The right hand was not savable, and doctors cut through the final few inches of skin, muscle, and tendons and left the stump wound open until a decision was made regarding a prosthetic. Even though the three outside fingers of his left hand were recovered at the mill scene, there was no hope of reattaching them with any function. The left-hand wound was also left open until a decision was made about a prosthetic. But doctors saw little hope of a partial artificial hand.

Sherry and Karen stayed at the hospital until late in the evening then took the Trueblood children home. The girls stayed the night with them, and the next day, they took them back to the hospital.

Jaine Trueblood had stayed the night at the hospital, but she was in a difficult position. Like most couples in the Carson/Stevenson area, especially those with children, they were a two-income household. Because of his injuries, Sam would not be going back to work at the mill anytime soon, if ever. Jaine wanted to stay with him at the hospital, but if she did not return to work, the family would have no income.

In addition to the living expenses, there were the medical expenses to consider. Things were changing in the medical field as lawmakers marched toward deregulation of hospitals, making costs rise. What little insurance the mill company provided would not be adequate to cover all costs, and if there was no income into the Trueblood household, the bills would not get paid.

She also wanted the children to remain in school so they did not fall behind.

Sherry, overhearing Jaine's conversations about her dilemma with her eldest daughter, wanted to find some way to help. She came up with a complicated plan.

First, on her next return to Carson, she went to as many businesses as she could to see if they would put donation jars in their facilities for the Trueblood family. Not one business rejected her request.

When she told Barry about this part of her plan, he said he would do the same in Stevenson, since he lived there. When word got out about what he was doing, other students from the school joined him, and soon they had jars in every business in town, both large and small.

Sherry also went to Jaine's employer, a small store in Carson, and offered to work for Jaine and hand over the wages to her. Jaine usually worked during the day, but the store owner did not want Sherry to miss school. However, he was moved by her offer and restructured the work schedule so Jaine's hours were now after school. The total hours during the week did not add up to what Jaine was working, so Sherry offered to also work on weekends.

Bob went to the mill management and convinced them to do something to help the Truebloods. Millwork was beginning to feel the effects of the growing environmentalist movement, calling for the reduction—if truth be told, the total elimination—of harvesting the nation's forests for lumber. As mill managers made reductions, that meant profits were reduced, and the Home Valley mill was barely making any money at all.

But management did offer $5,000 to Sam's medical expenses not covered by insurance.

Sherry also offered to help Bev Trueblood take care of her brother when she was not working at the store. Knowing her friend now had little time for much of anything else, Karen said she would help.

GORGE JUSTICE

Small towns are very tight-knit, hence the saying of Sherry's grandmother about their hometown in Wyoming. But the other side of that coin is that small towns generally take care of their own. Both aspects of those extremes were in play in Carson and Stevenson.

While the communities would have come out in support of the Trueblood family on its own, it was not lost on residents that it was Sherry Dyke who first got the ball rolling while the rest of the community was dealing with the shock of the incident. People were impressed that someone so new to the community would step forward so quickly in a crisis.

As the days went by since the accident, her efforts with the donation jars garnered immediate dividends. She had expected it to take weeks to raise $1,000. But within a few days, businesses were calling her and Barry to come empty the jars because they were overflowing. After they had made their rounds, they discovered $15,000 had been raised.

The money was given to Jaine, who promptly had Bev deposit it into her and Sam's joint bank account. It took a little longer the second time around, but within another week, businesses were calling again to have the jars emptied. This time, the total was about $16,000.

To acknowledge her efforts and to ease her burden, women and men in the community who had the time began to take over her work at the store on Jaine's behalf. It wasn't long before all of Jaine's regular day hours at the store were filled and there was no need for Sherry to cover her work hours. Carson neighbors of the Truebloods also started pitching in with the care of the Trueblood children, but Sherry made sure to spend time at their home a few days per week.

Once she was not working weekends, Sherry and Barry visited Jaine and Sam in the hospital one Saturday about a month after the accident. Jaine stayed at the hospital most of that time, with only a couple Sunday trips home to recharge and get fresh clothing.

Sam was improving slowly. He and the doctors decided against a prosthetic on the left hand, so the wound was closed and shaped. They did go ahead with plans for an artificial hand for his right arm, but that would take some time to adjust to once it was fitted. He was due to be discharged to continue his recovery at home soon.

He and Jaine could not say enough about how grateful they were to the community for its support. But it went further than that.

"You, young lady, we have been told, got all this started and so quickly," Jaine said to Sherry. "And you did so much yourself. There is no way we could ever repay you."

Sherry blushed. "I only did what I thought was right," she said.

"Oh, you did much more than that," Sam said from his hospital bed. It had been a long day of rehab, and he had been napping when Sherry and Barry came to the room. He had awoken when he felt his wife's grip on his mangled left hand disappear when she went to hug the young couple.

"You must be very proud of this one," Sam said to Barry. "But we know you were involved in all this too."

Barry looked at Sherry and beamed.

"Yes, I am very proud of her," he said then looked at the Truebloods. "But she did, and still does, much more than me."

"It doesn't matter who did what," Jaine said. "We are so very grateful."

"If there is ever anything either of you need, you come to us," Sam said. "We'll do our damnedest to make it happen."

* * *

As March rolled around in the Columbia Gorge, the temperature began to warm up and the rainy days became fewer. The hills on both sides of the mighty river took on a brighter and deeper blue-green color.

Students at schools in the Stevenson-Carson School District knew these were all signs that the summer break was coming. For seniors at Stevenson High School, they were also signs that they should be making decisions about their plans after graduation.

Both Sherry and Barry wanted to attend college. But since meeting the previous year and building such a strong bond, they were rethinking the preliminary plans they had been forming the previous summer.

Barry wanted to be a teacher and maybe even a basketball coach. That meant a school that had a curriculum designed for secondary education. Sherry had an interest in nursing but wasn't exactly sure that was the route she wanted to take.

They had, prior to Sam Trueblood's accident, studied the offerings of several colleges, both in Washington and Oregon. But so far, they had not made a decision about where they would go.

Complicating the issue was that now they wanted to be able to attend the same college. But finding one that offered both programs they needed and be within their financial ability was problematic.

Barry leaned toward Eastern Oregon State College, a small state school in La Grande, about 225 miles east. The school appealed to him because it was located in a town that, while larger than Stevenson and Carson combined, was not a large metropolitan area, with its associated problems. The small-town atmosphere appealed to him, as it did Sherry.

One weekend in March, they took a road trip to La Grande to look over the campus and talk to people in the admissions office. They were given a campus tour and gathered up all the information they could. They learned that the liberal arts school offered some prenursing courses but also a range of other options to choose from.

During the drive home, they decided this was where they wanted to continue their education together.

Shortly after Barry dropped Sherry off at home, Karen was knocking at the door. The two girls ran up to Sherry's room.

"I've got something to tell you," Karen said as they plopped down on Sherry's bed. She paused to let the suspense build up.

"So what is it?" Sherry finally exploded, seeing the glee on her friend's face.

"You are going to be the senior attendant at the prom," Karen said, spreading her arms and pulling Sherry to her in a big bear hug.

Sherry was dumbfounded.

"How did that happen?" she asked into Karen's dark hair covering her ear.

Karen released her from the hug and looked at her as if she had three heads.

"Don't you think that's really cool?" she asked. "I heard around school that the juniors on the committee were so impressed with the way you jumped in to help the Truebloods."

Sherry blushed and repeated what she had told Sam and Jaine in the hospital.

"Besides, I'm new here," she said. "This should have gone to someone who's been here longer…like you."

Karen waved a dismissive hand.

"I'm not interested in that," she said.

But from the conversations they'd had over the months since they met, Sherry knew better. Karen had talked about her disappointment at not being chosen as an attendant the year before and her disappointment at not being on the homecoming court. By the look on her friend's face, Karen knew what she was thinking.

"Oh, I know I told you I was disappointed about not being on other courts," she said. "But I've gotten past that. I've gotten used to the idea that it's not going to happen for me."

She threw her arms around Sherry again.

"But I am so happy for you," she said.

Sherry was grateful that her first friend in Carson was so gracious to be excited for her sudden popularity. But she wasn't excited for herself. This was not the kind of attention she wanted for herself. But at the same time, there was a part of her that was proud that she had been so accepted into her new community. It finally made her feel like she was a part of the community. She believed she could finally shed the horrible memories of what happened to her in Wyoming.

Chapter 6

But there was trouble on the horizon. Things began to change…for the worse.

It was not trouble between "Chip and Dale," as Barry and Sherry had come to be known around Stevenson and Carson. Their bond grew stronger with each passing day. They were solidifying plans to attend college together in the fall, and Sherry took on a part-time job at the store where Barry worked. It would transition to full-time through the summer. That would allow her to start adding to her savings so she would have spending money at college.

She and Barry had applied for and received grants and student loans to finance their higher education. They would live in the college dormitories, at least in their first year, possibly longer if it proved to be the better financial option.

They were busy getting all their ducks in a row for the fall, so busy, in fact, that they did not notice a subtle way some people, their peers and adults alike, were seeing them through different lenses.

Some of the boys at school looked at Sherry in a completely different way. Some were openly flirty, even though it was common knowledge she and Barry were dating exclusively. Once she started to notice it, it was clear that some of the flirtations were downright lecherous. It began to scare her.

Many of the girls began to stay away from Barry completely. Those who did give him looks made him feel like he was being viewed as a criminal.

It wasn't something that would come about naturally, especially after it seemed Sherry had really established herself in the community. There was just no apparent reason for the change in some of the schoolmates and some adults' attitude toward them. To get away from it, they stayed away from mostly everyone. They were almost never seen again except in school.

It wasn't a universal change though. They continued to have friends and supporters. But that circle seemed to shrink almost daily.

Karen Baxter remained loyal to them both. She had considered Sherry a real friend ever since the day she met her. She would do almost anything for her, and she couldn't understand why everyone was acting the way they were.

But one day she found out why. It was quite by accident. She was dressing after her physical education class, and she heard two other girls talking.

"But what kind of a person would do something like that?" asked one voice.

"You never know," said the other. "And I always thought she was a cool person. But I just can't see anyone denying life to a little child. That's terrible."

It didn't take much to figure out who and what they were talking about since Karen knew about Sherry's abortion and she had heard nothing about anyone else from the school—or community for that matter—who had done the same recently or in the near past. And she would have heard through the small-town grapevine. Not much was kept secret for long.

How pathetic it was to condemn someone for something like that, Karen thought. She wanted to tell Sherry what she had heard, but she remembered what Mary had told her. Then she thought of something else. She was the only one in town who had known about this before it had popped up. How did it get out? She hadn't told anyone. Had Mary told someone else? She did not even think that if

Sherry found out what was up and that she had known about it that she would get the blame. She did realize it later, but it was too late.

Sherry was walking out to Karen's car one afternoon after school, and Tim Kelley came up to her and put his arm around her.

Tim was a boy whom Sherry knew of but had rarely talked to. He was a bit on the rough side. Tim spent a lot of time in the high school principal's office and had been suspended once for smoking marijuana on school grounds. He had also been taken in by the police once, accused of shoplifting at a Stevenson store. But he was released when his mother, the wife of a long-haul truck driver who was rarely home, assured the police and store owner that Tim would be disciplined.

Whether he was or not was never certain.

"What say we go out tonight?" he asked Sherry as they walked.

"What?" Sherry asked, uncomfortable with the physical contact between them, but she didn't want to seem rude by removing his arm.

"I said we should go out tonight. What about it?"

"Sorry. You know I'm going steady with Barry."

"So what? He probably won't mind. After all, he knows about sharing the wealth and all that."

"What?"

"You know what I mean. I'm his friend. He'll share."

Sherry had heard Barry talk about Tim a time or two, but she never knew him to hang out with him. He certainly was not in the circle of friends Barry often talked about.

"I don't know what you mean by that. Share what?" Sherry asked as she quickened her pace.

"You."

The look on his face—that same lecherous look she was getting from other boys—told Sherry she had better get away from him. She ducked her shoulder down and out of his arm then began to jog toward Karen's car. Tim grabbed her arm.

"Come on. It gets kind of boring sleeping with just one guy all the time. Put some variety in your life."

"What? What are you talking about?"

"Don't play dumb with me. I've heard all about the baby you almost had in Wyoming and why you didn't have it. You don't have to sleep with one guy around here."

She pulled her arm out of his grasp and slapped him across the face. She turned and ran to Karen's car. Tim rubbed his jaw then waved a dismissive arm at her and walked away.

Sherry had to wait for Karen, and when she arrived, she saw that Sherry was crying.

"Hey, what's wrong?" she asked.

"Nothing. I just want to go home."

"But we were going to go to the pool," Karen protested.

"I just want to go home, please," Sherry sobbed.

"Sure." Karen took her straight home.

When she got home, she was crying even harder. Katrina saw her as she ran up to her room. Katrina went up to see what the matter was.

"What's wrong?" she asked when she reached her daughter's bed.

Sherry, who was lying on her stomach, sobbing into her pillow, turned on her side and looked up at her mother.

"They found out, Mom, they found out."

"Found out what?" Things had been going so well for the family she had almost forgotten why they were now in Carson, Washington.

"The abortion, dammit. And only one person could have told them, and I'm going to get that bitch."

Her tone was angry now. Katrina was surprised at her use of the word *bitch*. She had never heard Sherry curse before.

"Who?"

The answer was unexpected and shocking.

"Mary."

Mary had gotten a ride from school from a friend. She was let off at the end of the street, four blocks from the house. As she neared her home, she noticed a red Ford Mustang parked across the street from their house. She didn't pay much attention to it at first, but it seemed familiar. She just couldn't place it.

She went inside the house. Sherry and her mother were still upstairs in Sherry's room. Mary put her books on the table and went to the window. She looked a long time at the Mustang. The driver was looking at their house. He also looked familiar. He was wearing sunglasses and suddenly took them off. Mary immediately recognized him and jumped back from the window. It was Ted.

She had met him once while Sherry was dating him and took an instant dislike to him. Mary had also heard plenty about the young man through the small-town Wyoming grapevine. He had a reputation of someone who had to be in control of all situations. She had also heard that he had a temper and it flared when he did not get his way.

Mary had to find her mother. She wasn't in the kitchen, but as Mary came out, Katrina came down the stairs. Before she was could say anything, Mary was told to go to the kitchen. Her mother said she wanted to talk to her. When her mother followed her into the kitchen and Mary turned to face her, Mary knew something was terribly wrong.

She sat down across the table from her mother. She waited for her to say something. Katrina thought for a moment, trying to gather what she was going to say. This would be difficult. Finally, she looked her daughter in the eye.

"Did you tell anyone about Sherry's abortion?" she asked.

Mary's first reaction was surprise. She had heard nothing of it from anyone. But all at once, it hit her. The Mustang, its driver—she put the pieces together quickly.

"No, Mom, but I think I know who did," she answered excitedly.

Katrina was surprised at this and followed as her daughter ran into the living room. She joined Mary at the window.

"Look."

Katrina gasped in surprised recognition. There was Ted still sitting in his car across the street, looking at the house. While he had no problem when Mary was staring at him through the window, he was not excited to recognize the other face that appeared next. Sherry's parents were never accepting of their daughter dating him. While

Ted was filled with bravado when he was dealing with someone who was easily intimidated, Bob and Katrina Dyke did not fit that mold.

He fired the Mustang to life and roared down the street.

"Stay here," Katrina said and bolted up the stairs.

Sherry was in tears after her mother had told her about Ted.

"What am I going to do now, Mom?" she sobbed. "I thought I'd gotten away from it. Now they all know, and Ted has come to get me."

"You don't know he's here to get you," Katrina tried to soothe her daughter.

"But what else would he be here for?" she wailed. "And watching our house. He's going to get me, Mom."

"Don't worry, dear. He'll never get you. We'll see to that."

This seemed to make her stop crying some, and Katrina was relieved.

"I want to apologize to Mary," Sherry said as she wiped the tears away. "Could you please send her up?"

Katrina nodded and left the room.

Mary was still at the window when her mother came down. She was looking up the street to see if she could see where Ted had gone. But he had disappeared up another street. Katrina told her that Sherry wanted to talk to her. Mary went slowly up the stairs.

Mary stood in the doorway of the bedroom she and her sister shared. She wasn't sure what to expect. Sherry was sitting on her bed with her back to the door. She hadn't seen Mary standing there.

"Mom said you wanted to talk to me," Mary finally said.

Sherry slowly turned to face her. Mary saw the tear tracks down her cheeks that no amount of wiping would take them away. She could see more tears forming in her sister's eyes.

"Yes," Sherry began. "I wanted to tell you I was sorry for what I said about you. I thought for sure you had told everybody."

"What did you say about me? You never said anything to me."

"I didn't say it to you. I'm just really very sorry."

"It's all right. I was the only one who knew, so it would have had to have been me if he wasn't here," Mary said. "What are you going to do now? Does Barry know?"

"No. He doesn't know anything about that," Sherry answered. "I don't know what I'm going to do. I guess I'll just have to stay here and take it. We only have a couple of months of school left, and then I'll be working during the summer until Barry and I go to college."

"What about Barry?" Mary asked. "Are you going to tell him?"

"I don't know. I just don't know how he'll react when I tell him about…"

She couldn't finish through the flood of tears that now came again.

Mary left the room. She knew Sherry wanted to be alone.

Sherry had not told Barry about the abortion, but he would eventually know. Sherry wanted to tell him herself, but fate wouldn't allow it to happen that way. He found out the very next day.

Barry was dressing after his PE class when Bob Masters walked over to where he was sitting and sat down next to him.

"You got any off her yet?" he asked.

"What?"

"I said, have you got any off her yet?" Bob answered.

"Who?"

"Who?" Bob laughed. "Sherry, that's who."

"I don't see how that is any of your business."

"Well, I thought you weren't gonna let that dude from where she's from show you up," Bob said. "Maybe I was wrong."

He started to get up and leave, but Barry grabbed his shirt.

"What do you mean by that?"

Barry could get very hostile at times, and Bob knew it. This looked like it could become one of those times.

"Take it easy," Bob said, trying unsuccessfully to break Barry's grip on his shirt. "This dude just got her pregnant, that's all. And he's in town too."

Barry let him go and hurriedly dressed and left.

After school, he sat in his car waiting for Sherry. He just couldn't believe it. Sherry hadn't told him anything about it, and they always shared their secrets, no matter how bad they were. He was going to ask her about it nevertheless.

When she appeared at the front entrance of the school, he got out of the car and went to meet her and start right in. But he decided that was not the time or place.

The drive to Carson was made in silence. Sherry wanted to tell him, but she was scared of how he might react. Barry wanted to wait to say something. He had to get it straight in his head what he was going to say. Sherry tried to start a conversation a few times, but Barry dismissed her questions with quick, short answers. When they arrived at Sherry's house and she leaned over to kiss him goodbye, he turned away.

"I want to talk to you," he said.

The tone of his voice made Sherry sit straight up. She got very worried very quickly.

"What about?" she asked shakily. She was so afraid to lose him. He represented her security when he was near her.

"About when you were in Wyoming." She stiffened in the seat. "Did you get pregnant?"

The shock of his blunt question sent a shiver through her whole body. She was expecting something, but the bluntness of his questions caught her off guard. She could feel the tears starting to form in her eyes. But she couldn't lie to him.

"Yes." Her voice quivered, elongating the word and making it sound like a vibrato. "Why?"

"What happened to the baby?" he asked.

She was certain he already knew the answer but told him anyway. "I had an abortion."

"Why didn't you tell me?" he asked, still in an unemotional tone.

"I thought you would be like everyone is now that they know about it and hate me because I had an abortion," she answered, fighting back the tears.

It was a fight she could not win, and she broke down and sobbed openly and loudly. Barry reached over with his right hand and lifted her chin and turned her face toward him. He then leaned over and kissed her quivering lips, soaked with her tears.

"Sherry, if you had an abortion, you must have had a good reason, and if you think it was a good enough reason, I won't question it," Barry said, this time with love and care in his voice.

Sherry began to sob harder.

"I love you very much. Nothing will change that," he continued.

Sherry tried to control her crying, but it took some time. She had gone from being sure Barry would turn against her to hearing him say none of it mattered to him. She wanted so much to believe him, to know that there was someone who would look past her terrible secret.

"Now is there anything else you want to tell me?" Barry asked.

She wiped most of the tears from her cheeks and looked over at him.

"The guy that got me pregnant is here, and I think he's after me," she said slowly, the fear taking over her expression.

"Don't worry about it," Barry said. "I won't let anyone do anything to you."

Suddenly, Sherry was seized with an overwhelming sense of relief. Not that she felt entirely safe from Ted but that she had unburdened herself of the secret to Barry, and he had not turned on her or treated her just like another lay because of his knowledge of her past.

She broke out in tears again, but this time, they were tears of joy. Barry hugged her tight against him, and she knew she had someone who loved her, cared about her, and would not judge her.

Chapter 7

While Barry's love and support gave Sherry something good to look forward to, she found she would have to lean on him more.

As the days passed, most people in Carson and Stevenson, with the exception of Karen and her parents and a few others, bought into the rumors being generated as the truth of Sherry's past in Wyoming came to light. It seemed that she was looked upon as a promiscuous woman by all the women and some of the men. Most of the rest of the men looked at her like the village bicycle, on which everyone could get a ride. She knew those men would see her as only that and try to get her to bed with them whenever they could.

She stayed home most of the time, but people did get a chance to harass her whenever she did leave the house. The attitude toward her from both communities clouded the news Karen had given her about being picked as an attendant for the prom. There had been discussion among the junior class, which prepared the event, about replacing her. But school administrators would not allow a replacement on such short notice.

With the event just days away, Sherry considered skipping it altogether. But Barry talked her out of it.

"I think we should go just like we planned," he had told her. "You need to show them that you're not going to buckle under their harassment."

She appreciated his support. But things were getting worse, and one night, two days after Barry convinced her to not skip the prom, her bad dream turned into a horrifying nightmare.

She was walking home from the store not long after darkness had covered the Washington river town. She wasn't more than one hundred yards from her house when a big, strong hand grabbed her from behind and another hand clamped over her mouth. She dropped the sack of things she was carrying and tried to look around to see who it was. But the viselike grip would not allow her to move her head at all. She started to struggle, but whoever it was who had her was very strong. She was dragged to a car alongside the road and thrown into the back seat.

Before she could scream, another hand from someone already in the car clamped over her mouth. A bandana was placed over her eyes and tied in the back clearly by a third person. Not a word was spoken by any of them as the car roared down the road. It continued for a while, and Sherry was certain they had left town. She recognized the whine of the tires as they left the pavement and crossed the Wind River Canyon bridge. Because of that, she knew they were going north.

The car did not go very far past the bridge before turning off the highway onto a dirt side road. They bumped their way along it for what seemed to Sherry like quite a distance.

Finally, they came to a stop, and Sherry was thrown out violently. She was dragged to the rear of the car and pinned to the trunk by two of her abductors. She then heard the voice of the third person right in front of her.

"You're not going to get away this time."

She recognized Ted's voice. She started to scream as loud as she could. He slapped her across the face.

"Scream all you want to," he said. "No one will hear you."

She could feel him begin to unbutton her pants. She kicked out blindly with her right leg but missed connecting with anything but air. Ted hit her again, this time a swift jab with his closed fist. She felt her jaw go numb.

"You better knock that shit off, bitch."

He had unbuttoned and unzipped her pants and yanked them down to her ankles. He reached up and pulled her panties down then pulled both off her left leg and threw them aside, still around her right ankle. She tried to kick out again with her left foot, which still had her shoe on despite Ted yanking her pants and panties over the foot, but she again missed. The person on her left holding her against the car truck hooked his foot around her ankle and pinned her leg against the car's bumper.

Sherry felt Ted's hands grab the front of her V-neck T-shirt and pull outward. The tearing fabric and the cool air against her bare torso told her it had been torn completely down the front. She then felt Ted's hands grab her bra and rip it apart in the front.

Still blindfolded, she felt the people holding her tightened their grip on her shoulders with one arm, and she felt their other hands on her thighs trying to spread her legs. Sherry squeezed as hard as she could to keep them together. She felt Ted's fist plunge into her belly. The breath poured out of her lungs, and the next few minutes were cloudy and gray.

Ted put his hands on the truck on either side of Sherry and had his feet back a step to give him leverage, and he thrust himself inside her before she put up any more resistance. He was driving upward so hard it felt like her insides were being ripped apart. He had orgasmed once and was about to a second time when Sherry worked up enough strength to give one more gesture of defiance. When she had lost her breath, those holding her had let go of her legs. Sherry slammed her legs together, catching him on the forward thrust with his testicles swinging forward, just as he came inside her. It was like slapping two boards together with his balls in between.

He jerked his already limp penis out of her, moaning in pain. Just as he started to take a step backward, Sherry swung her right leg up blindly and, despite her pants and panties wrapped around her ankle, connected between his legs. She then slumped down in near collapse, supported only by the two people on either side of her. Ted dropped to his knees, grabbing at his crotch.

"You dirty fucking bitch!" Ted screamed after feeling the pain start to subside.

He rubbed his aching crotch and pulled up his pants and fastened them. He came forward with a fist deep into Sherry's belly again. He followed that with several violent slugs to the face. She felt the blood begin to flow from her nose, lip, and left cheek.

Ted continued the assault on her head. He finally stepped back, but it wasn't over for Sherry. The two at her sides picked her up bodily and threw her onto a pile of rocks. She landed roughly on her right arm and felt it collapse in several places. The trio then went to her and kicked her repeatedly from head to toe. One of them stomped down on her legs, and she felt them break.

It was then the attackers backed off. She could hear them breathing heavily for a few minutes, then silence, until the car engine started, and she heard it drive away. She knew they had left her to die.

Sherry was barely conscious, but she did not want to black out. After lying there for a few moments, she rolled over on her belly. Reaching up with her intact arm, she pulled off the blindfold. Through her clouded mind, she took in her surroundings. She was in a small clearing, about the size of half a gymnasium floor. Next to the small pile of rocks she was on was what appeared to be an old campfire pit that had not been used recently. On the other side of the clearing, she made out a small road. Slowly, painfully she used her good arm, and she pulled up her panties and pants, buttoning the pants with much difficulty. She then began to drag herself to the road's edge.

But which way should she go? She lay there for a while trying to make a decision. Suddenly, she heard the familiar whine of tires on the Wind River Canyon bridge. It was coming from her left, she was certain. So that was the way she began to drag herself along the dirt road.

Sherry could feel the blood still flowing from her nose, lip, and cheek. From time to time, using the edges of her torn shirt, she dabbed at the wounds. The flow never stopped completely, but it did begin to slow some.

The trek down the road was a long one. Sherry had no concept of time, so she had no clue how long it took. Because they were broken, her legs were not helpful; they were just deadweight. As she moved forward, dirt from the road started to work its way inside the front of her pants. A few times the pants snagged on a rock or tree root and she had to use her good arm to free herself. Because her shirt and bra were torn open at the front, her breasts and belly took some punishment as they were dragged along. Thankfully, the road was used enough during the daylight hours that there was a thin layer of fine dirt and dust, so there was some cushion.

The trouble was, she was physically weak at the beginning of the journey, and with each foot she pulled herself forward, she was getting weaker. Several times she stopped to rest. But it was only enough to get her a few more yards before she had to rest again.

Just when she thought she could not go any farther, she felt something different when she put her arm forward for the next drag forward. It was hard, and there was no soft dirt cushion. She pulled forward and extended her arm again. The same hard surface. Two more drags and Sherry finally went totally unconscious, not really knowing that she had reached the highway and lay halfway into the northbound lane.

* * *

Jim and Helen Brewster were driving north on the road out of Carson very early in the morning. The sun was just starting to lighten the night sky as they neared the Wind River Canyon bridge.

Jim and Helen had been married sixteen years. There wasn't a day that went by that they weren't arguing about something or other. In the past couple of months, they had been trying to fix their marriage. That was what they were doing this particular day. Jim thought it would be a good idea to go driving, away from town and their two children, and talk things out.

Jim had just crossed the Wind River Canyon bridge and driven about fifty yards when his headlights illuminated something partially in his lane of travel ahead. At first, he thought it was a deer or some other animal that had been hit by a passing car. But as he slowed his car and got closer, he could see it was a human body. He brought the car to a stop within about five yards of the body and turned on his emergency flashers.

"Stay here," he told Helen and got out of the car.

He ran over to the body, which was lying facedown. He carefully turned it over. A cold chill ran through his body as he recognized Sherry Dyke.

He quickly checked for a pulse. Initially, he could not find one. But he tried again and found a very weak beat. He saw she had a trickle of blood coming from her nose, and there was dried blood on her lip and cheek. There was also some dried blood mixed with dirt on her bare chest and on the shirt and bra that had been torn down the front. He also noticed her right arm looked slightly misshapen.

He ran to his car and grabbed his jacket.

"Bring the first aid kit out to me," he instructed Helen. He noticed the questioning look on her face and said as he headed back to the injured girl, "It's Sherry Dyke. She's hurt real bad."

When he got back to Sherry, Jim covered her exposed upper torso with his jacket. Helen ran to the opposite side of the prone figure and handed her husband the first aid kit. He applied a bandage to the small cut on her cheek and put a small wad of cotton in her left nostril to stop the small flow of blood.

Jim then went to her feet and carefully removed her shoes, leaving the ankle socks on. While doing so, he noticed both her legs seemed more flexible than they should have been.

Because the nearest telephone was back in town, Jim decided they needed to take her to get medical attention. He instructed Helen to move the car up so they would not have to carry her far. Once it was in place, they both carefully lifted her and placed her on the back seat. They got into the car and turned back toward Carson.

Washington State Patrolman Harry Holister was patrolling alone that morning. He had stopped on the south side of the highway at the western junction from Carson. He intended to just drink a cup of coffee at the small café there. As he got out of the car, he heard the roar of a car engine and looked up in time to see Jim and Helen's car roar onto the highway from the road that came from Carson, running through the stop sign. There was no need for radar;

he knew they were speeding. The driver had to be drunk or crazy, Holister thought.

But Harry saw something that changed his mind. The car had its emergency flashers on. This indicated to Harry that something was definitely wrong, and it wasn't a drunk or crazy driver.

He jumped in his cruiser and gunned it down the road. He caught up with the Brewsters quickly and passed them. Once he was in position in front of them, he turned on his lights and siren. He had no clear idea of the problem, but his guess was that someone was injured and was being taken to the medical clinic in Stevenson.

* * *

Sherry's eyes fluttered open. She fought to clear the haze from her vision and brain.

Once she was seeing and thinking more clearly, she tried to focus on her surroundings. She was lying flat on her back, and the first thing she saw was a white ceiling.

Before looking around, she took in the antiseptic smell. She remembered it vividly from her visits to Sam Trueblood at the hospital in White Salmon and later in Hood River, across the Columbia in Oregon. She tried to sit up, but her arms wouldn't move to support her. She tried to raise herself using just her stomach muscles, but she was too weak. Her movements sent sharp pain ripping through her whole body and head. She sagged back onto the bed.

Suddenly, she heard her mother at her left side.

"Sherry, can you hear me?"

She turned her head slowly and saw her parents sitting by her bed.

"Yes," she said. Pain tore through her face.

"Don't try to talk too much," Bob said. "Just nod or shake your head."

"Do you know who did this to you?" Katrina asked.

Sherry nodded weakly, and Katrina saw a pained look cross her face.

"Was it Ted?"

Again, she nodded, tears starting to pool up in her eyes. Bob reached out and wiped her eyes with a tissue.

"Was he alone?"

Sherry slowly shook her head.

"How bad am I hurt?" Sherry managed.

"Please, Sherry, wait until you feel stronger," Bob told her before his wife could answer. Katrina looked at her husband, flashing a question with her eyes. He nodded vigorously in response. She then turned to her daughter. "We'll be back later to see how you are doing," she told Sherry.

It was puzzling to Sherry that her parents would leave just after she woke up.

After they left the room, Barry walked in and sat next to the bed.

"I'm glad you're awake," he told Sherry, lightly rubbing her injured cheek with the back of his hand. When she winced, he pulled his hand away and put it in his lap with the other. "We were all afraid you weren't going to make it. It's been a long couple of days waiting."

"A long couple of days?" Sherry asked and again felt the pain in her face.

"Yes. Didn't your parents tell you? You have been unconscious for at least forty-eight hours, maybe more."

She was too shocked to say anything. He went on.

"You lost so much blood the doctors were afraid you might die," Barry explained. "Terry and I gave two pints of blood each. We were the only ones with your type that were able to donate."

Sherry had a rush of excitement, mixed with concern.

"Terry's here?" again her face stung with pain.

"Yes, he was," Barry said. "He got a three-day pass when he heard, but then he had to get back to base, so he left this morning."

She tried to smile, but the pain intensified.

"Why is it...," she began, but Barry stopped her. He handed her a pad of paper and a pen from the bedside table. She wrote on it as best she could with her left hand and gave it to him.

"Why is it so painful when I talk?"

"Your lip was cut pretty bad at the corner of your mouth, all the way through," Barry told her. "There are about eight stitches."

She took the pad and pen back.

"What else has happened to me?"

Barry thought for a moment. Had her parents told her? If not, should he be the one to do it? He finally decided to be honest with her.

"I don't know all of it," he said. "Both your legs are broken, and your right arm is broken. You already know about your lip. There are some scrapes and scratches on your upper body…"

Barry stopped in midsentence by the look of pain on Sherry's face.

"You don't want to hear this?" he half asked and half said.

"No, I do want to hear…," Sherry started to answer but then grimaced even more, and her left hand went to her belly.

"What's wrong?" Barry had jumped up and was leaning over her.

"My stomach," she cried.

Barry sprinted out of the room and returned immediately with a nurse. She checked Sherry's midsection as she continued to cry out in pain.

"You'll have to leave now," the nurse said to Barry without looking at him, her focus riveted on the patient.

"What is it?" Barry asked.

"I don't know for sure, but it could be internal bleeding," the nurse said. "Now go!"

Barry backed out of the room and nearly bumped into a doctor coming in. Barry needed to catch Sherry's parents and bring them back. He caught up with them halfway to Home Valley. When he told them about Sherry's abdominal pain, they all turned right back around and headed to the hospital.

The hours seemed to transform into days and weeks for Bob and Katrina and the rest of their children as they sat in the hospital waiting room. Sherry had been in surgery almost three hours now. Barry had gone downtown to get them all something to eat. None of them had eaten since Sherry had been brought to the hospital.

Jim and Helen Brewster came to see how Sherry was doing.

"She's been taken back into surgery," Bob told them.

Katrina sat beside him, trying as hard as she could to keep from crying. She was very near to losing the battle.

"We're really very sorry," Jim said.

"Thank you," Bob said. "We'll be forever grateful to you for bringing her in."

"We couldn't let her lay there like that," Helen said. "Who knows how long it would have taken an ambulance to get there."

"But others around here would have left her there," Bob said bitterly. "Thank you."

Jim started to protest. He wanted to defend the "people around here." But Bob was right, and Jim knew it all too well. He himself was one of those "people around here" at one time. But the sight of Sherry lying in that road near death melted his heart.

The Brewsters said their goodbyes and left. Katrina held up until they were gone. Then she broke down and cried in Bob's arms.

Barry had not yet returned with food when the doctor came to where Bob and Katrina were sitting. He was young and looked tired. He pulled off his surgical gloves, still stained with Sherry's blood, and fell into a chair across from Sherry's parents. The sight of the bloody gloves had Katrina's heart pumping harder. The doctor noticed her staring at them and stuffed the gloves into a pocket, looking a little embarrassed.

"Mr. and Mrs. Dyke, your daughter is out of danger for the moment," he said wearily.

"For the moment?" Bob asked.

"Yes, for the moment," the doctor answered. "We were able to stop the internal bleeding. But what I'm most worried about are her legs."

The doctor leaned forward in his chair, putting his elbows on his knees and burying his head in his hands. For a few seconds, he stayed that way, then he looked up at the Dykes.

"As she dragged herself along, dirt got down into her pants and eventually worked their way to her legs. Those breaks, unlike her arm, had jagged bones breaking the skin to create open wounds. A lot of that dirt was pushed into those wounds."

He let that sink in for Sherry's parents for a few seconds.

"There is no way to know if we got it all cleaned out," he explained. "There is still a high risk of infection."

Bob and Katrina sat in shock for a moment, and the doctor said nothing more.

"Can we speak to her?" Katrina finally asked.

"She is still under sedation, but you can as soon as she is conscious," the doctor said, standing up. "That should be in about a half hour."

Katrina was dozing in the chair next to her bed when Sherry stirred. She had gotten the go-ahead from the lead nurse to wait in her daughter's room, but only one person was allowed in until she was conscious. Sherry opened her eyes and turned her head to the right. She saw her mother there and started to speak.

"Don't talk, Sherry," her mother said. "I'll be right back."

Katrina went to the door and motioned. Sherry had closed her eyes but reopened them when her parents returned to the right side of her bed. Suddenly, she was aware of someone's hand covering her left hand. She rotated her head to the left and saw Barry sitting next to her. He gripped her hand, but she was too weak to do the same. She gave him as big a smile as she could, still feeling the pain at the corner of her mouth.

Barry leaned over her and kissed her cheek.

"You're going to be all right," he assured her.

"Will you be all right?" Katrina asked. "Your father and I have to get home soon."

Sherry nodded, looking at her parents, wondering why they would need to leave her so soon.

"We'll be back as soon as we can," Katrina assured her.

Barry was miserable and angry as he sat and looked at Sherry lying there on her bed. She couldn't move much and couldn't talk without pain. Her pain flowed into him. He couldn't sit and look at her in such pain and so helpless. He looked away.

"What's wrong?" Sherry asked, risking the pain.

"I'm just upset over what happened," he answered, still looking away.

There was more to it than that, but he could not tell her. As much as they shared their secrets with each other, he couldn't tell her this. What he had on his mind was taking the law into his own hands. He knew she would protest if he told her.

Barry did not want Sherry or anyone else to stop him. Someone had done this to his Sherry, and he was going to see that they were punished. He needed to get her to tell him as many details as she could remember.

"Do you know who did this to you?"

Sherry nodded.

"Who was it?"

Sherry looked at him for some sort of clue of what he was thinking, but there was none.

"Ted Brennen," she finally answered. "He's the guy I told you about."

Barry leaned over and kissed her then stood up to leave.

"I've got to go," he said. "I'll come and see you first thing I can tomorrow, okay?"

Sherry looked at him with pleading in her eyes.

"Don't go after him, Barry, please," she begged.

He just looked back at her. The sight of her lying on that hospital bed, helpless and in pain, made his anger rise. He turned and left the room without another word. Once outside the hospital, he set about to do what he believed he had to do. The first thing he had to do was find Ted.

Chapter 8

Bob and Katrina left Sherry's room, but they did not go home. They had unfinished business to attend to that was interrupted prior to Sherry's surgery. They went to the Skamania County sheriff's office in Stevenson and filed charges against Ted. A warrant was issued for his arrest.

The trouble was, no one knew where he was.

However, because the Dykes knew what kind of car he drove, they provided that information to the desk sergeant they spoke to. No, they didn't know the license plate number. But because it was most likely still registered in Wyoming, officers contacted the Wyoming State Police and the state's Department of Transportation and got the plate number.

After checking with area rentals and motels, they found where the car was listed. Four deputies were dispatched to the small six-room Home Valley motel where it was learned he had been staying.

Barry gunned his Grand Prix down the highway. The thought of Sherry lying in that hospital drove him onward. After driving to Stevenson, he had talked to Mary at the high school to see just what and who he was looking for. She told him what Ted drove. She also gave him a clue as to where he might be found. She had heard talk at school from some of the guys Ted had met since coming to Carson.

They talked about a guy from Wyoming who was living somewhere along the river, but not in Stevenson.

Barry knew nothing about Bob and Katrina's trip to the sheriff's station and the warrant for Ted's arrest. All he had on his mind was vengeance for what he had done to his Sherry.

As he passed the little red café at the Carson junction, a red Mustang roared past him going in the opposite direction. Barry saw the Wyoming license plate and made a high-speed U-turn in the middle of the narrow highway and sped after him. Three sheriff's patrol cars came roaring up behind him, lights and sirens on. But Barry didn't slow down.

The caravan of speeding cars roared through Stevenson without even slowing down. Barry knew where Ted was going—the Bridge of the Gods. He would try to lose his pursuers and get on Interstate 80. Barry wondered if Ted knew it was a toll bridge.

As they approached the bridge, Barry saw the headlights of a truck ahead. Ted didn't even slow down. Ted cut across the path of the oncoming truck, and Barry followed suit, just missing the grillwork of the fully loaded Peterbilt logger by inches. The truck driver slammed on his brakes, and the trailer fishtailed. When the smoke cleared from the screeching tires, the cab and trailer completely blocked the approach to the bridge.

Barry glanced in his rearview mirror and saw the police cars could not get through. But up ahead, he saw red-and-blue flashing lights. Two Oregon State Police cruisers were at the toll gate.

Ted, not slowing at all, crashed through the toll barrier and hit one of the OSP cars, spinning it around. The two state troopers who were stationed in front of the car were barely able to jump clear before the collision. Ted's car plowed into the embankment on the turn coming off the bridge.

Barry stopped his car at the toll booth and jumped out. He ran to Ted's Mustang and yanked the driver's side door open. Before Ted, who was still a little dazed, could do anything, Barry grabbed his shirt front and pulled him from the car.

"You son of a bitch!" Barry screamed. "You've had it!"

Barry landed a blow on Ted's jaw. Ted fell to the ground. As he was trying to scramble to his feet, Barry kicked him in the face, and he went down again.

Barry heard the sirens wailing from the bridge. The sheriff's deputies from Washington had gotten through. He grabbed Ted by the hair and jerked him to his feet.

"I'd love to kill you," he said, with his nose nearly touching Ted's. "But I think it will be more pleasant if I turn you over to the police so you can rot and suffer in jail."

A police car skidded to a halt by his side just as the two OSP troopers came running to the scene after crawling back up the bank from where they dived after their cruiser was smashed into. Barry threw Ted onto the hood of the sheriff's car. The deputies jumped out and grabbed Ted. One of the troopers grabbed Barry.

"Let him go," said one of the deputies as his partner mirandized Ted then handcuffed him.

"I'm going to sue you for assault and battery, and you'll rot and suffer alongside me, you fucker!" Ted hollered.

The deputy squeezed the handcuffs a little tighter.

"Did you understand your rights as I explained them to you?" he asked Ted. "Especially the one about remaining silent?"

"Yes, asshole," he answered.

The deputy roughly shoved him into the back seat of the cruiser, making sure to protect his head as he sat down to keep it from bumping the car roof. Ted tried to shake the deputy's hand off his head, only to smack his noggin against the rear window post. The deputy shook his head and smiled as he got into the driver's seat.

* * *

Barry sat next to Sherry's hospital bed with a newspaper in his lap. The headline hinted at the story: BOYFRIEND OF RAPED GIRL CAPTURES SUSPECT ALONE.

"How are you feeling?" he asked Sherry.

"I'm fine," she answered, but she looked upset.

"What's wrong?" he asked. Then he added, "I can tell something is bothering you."

"I asked you not to go after him," she answered after a pause. "Why did you?"

"Because it really tore me up seeing you lying there and him running loose." Barry could feel the anger rising in himself again.

"Why do you still stay with me after I cause you so much pain?" Sherry asked, turning her head away from him in a vain attempt to hide her tears.

"Because I love you, Sherry," Barry said softly, trying to push his anger back deep inside his mind.

She turned to look at him again. He stood up and leaned over her, giving her a tight hug. They both burst into tears.

The doctors said she was improving, but that was not easing Barry's mind. The way she had acted when he was with her told him otherwise. He hoped his suspicions were wrong, but they weren't.

Two days after Ted's capture, she fell into painful convulsions and was rushed to surgery again. This time, it was four and a half hours before the young doctor emerged from the operating room and went to Bob and Katrina. Again, his manner startled them. This time, there was reason.

"There have been complications," he told them. Bob leaned forward in his chair while Katrina collapsed into tears.

"What kind of complications?" Bob demanded.

The doctor looked at this father with sadness in his eyes. He had no children of his own, but he could see in Bob the anguish and anxiety mixed with anger that was tearing him apart. This part of his job was the worst, and he was struggling to deal with it.

"We had to remove the spleen," he explained. "It was completely destroyed by one of the blows she took."

Katrina wailed.

The young doctor realized he had been too blunt.

"I'm sorry to have upset you," he said. "This is not a life-threatening situation."

He explained that while the spleen was an important organ that helps filter blood, there are other organs, the lymphatic system and liver, that step in and do the work in a spleen's absence.

"Most people live very normal lives without a spleen," he explained. "She'll just have to make sure she's vaccinated, and she'll have to take daily antibiotics."

Katrina and Bob looked only slightly relieved. But Bob was quick to recall there was apparently more to talk about.

"You said complications, plural," he said to the doctor. "What else?"

"She also needs more blood," the doctor said apologetically.

Barry was standing next to Bob.

"I'm ready to give more," he said without hesitation. Bob looked up at him.

"We can't ask you to do that again," he told Barry.

"Mr. Dyke, I will give all the blood I have if it will save Sherry," Barry shot back with a firmness that impressed Bob and the doctor. They all looked to the doctor.

"Will he be able to give enough?" Katrina asked. "Should we have our son come down?"

The doctor thought for a moment, doing some calculations in his head.

"I believe this young man can supply what we need," he said, looking at Barry.

"You take whatever you need," Barry said.

"Then let's get to work," the doc said and led Barry away.

* * *

Ted faced the Skamania County judge during his arraignment. A public defender stood beside him. He faced charges of reckless driving, speeding, evading police officers, and reckless endangerment.

His attorney had encouraged him to plead no contest to the charges. His advice was that the chances were he would get probation or, in the worst-case scenario, there would be a small amount of jail time. He assured Ted if there were any jail time, it would be in the county facility and would not be that long or harsh.

Ted saw the wisdom in the advice and agreed.

As it turned out, he faced a judge who had a low tolerance level for endangering others on the road and disrespect for law enforcement.

"You are sentenced to spend sixty days in the county jail, the maximum I can give you under state law," the judge said. "There will be no chance for early release."

Ted looked at the attorney with fire in his eyes.

"Just be happy you didn't have a DUI in there," the attorney said as he packed his briefcase. "You'd probably be in the state pen in Walla Walla."

"Fuck you, asshole!" Ted yelled as the bailiffs led him away and the lawyer walked out of the small courtroom.

* * *

Weeks went by, and Sherry began to improve. Once she was able to get out of her hospital bed and get some exercise, even if it was in a wheelchair while her legs healed, her physical condition and emotional state continued to improve.

During that time, the first signs of yet another change began to grip the towns of Carson and Stevenson. Sherry began to have visitors in the hospital who had turned away from her and some who had never even paid attention to her before.

On the day of graduation at Stevenson High School, Sherry was loaded into her wheelchair and taken from the hospital. She was not told where she was going, but after they went past both roads that led to Carson, she knew she wasn't going home. Once in Stevenson, she could tell they were heading for the high school. She was quite confused when her parents, with a hand on each handle of the wheelchair, rolled her into the gymnasium. They took her to a spot right behind Barry. The cap and gown looked good on him.

The ceremony was long and painful for Sherry. She knew she would not graduate with her classmates; she had missed too much class time.

When Barry's name was called and he received his diploma, Sherry managed a light applause with her right arm still in a cast.

As the last name was called and the final diploma given, the school principal stepped to the podium. Sherry was a little confused as the traditional throwing of caps did not take place.

"As you all know," the principal began, "there is yet another member of this graduating class. But she has missed the final two months of school."

He looked down at Sherry and smiled, savoring the look on her face as she realized he was talking about her.

"We, the faculty and administration, took a vote," he went on. "Based on her past grades before transferring to Stevenson and her work the first seven months this year, we unanimously agreed that this student would have passed her courses with flying colors."

Sherry was still trying to make sense of the sudden attention being paid to her when the principal concluded.

"Therefore, Sherry Dyke, come forward and receive your diploma," he said.

Sherry felt her heart quicken, and she was suddenly a little lightheaded. While she had figured out it was her he was describing, his last pronouncement was quite surprising. She had already been asking her parents to look into some type of summer schooling.

She looked back at both her parents in turn as they pushed her toward the platform on which the diplomas were given. They were both smiling down on her, enormous pride glowing within them.

Sherry was wheeled to the front of the platform where the principal was waiting for her. He put the diploma in her lap while shaking her left hand. He then pulled a felt pen from his suit jacket pocket.

"May I?" he asked, gesturing toward the cast on her right arm. She smiled through the tears and nodded. He bent down and signed the plaster encasing her healing arm. Under his name, he wrote, "To a very courageous woman. Good luck." It was the first signature outside of her immediate family and Barry to sign any of her three casts.

The principal returned to the platform and began to speak. Sherry wondered why her parents were not wheeling her back to her place in the crowd.

"Will Barry Walker please step forward," the principal said.

Barry stood and walked proudly to the podium. From behind the podium, he pulled a large silver trophy.

"I have been chosen by the senior class as the presenter of this award," he said. "It is a very special trophy. It, and another one like it, was purchased with senior class funds. The other trophy will be a traveling one, presented not every year but whenever each senior class deems it appropriate."

Sherry had already guessed that she was going to be a recipient again. She began to cry.

"This trophy will be awarded to the first recipient," he said, looking over the hardware. Then for the first time during his speech, he looked at Sherry. There was a tear in his eye and a smile on his face as wide as the Columbia River.

"The first recipient of the Sherry Dyke Award for Courage is its namesake Sherry Dyke," he announced to no one's surprise.

Barry carried the trophy off the platform and set it in front of Sherry. He leaned down and kissed her, and that was when the crowd's polite applause erupted into a thunderous standing ovation.

As Barry returned to his seat and Sherry remained in front of the platform, the principal began to speak again.

"Sherry Dyke has endured in the last two months a tremendous amount of pain and agony," he said. "But through it all, she has hung on." He paused for a moment, trying to maintain his composure.

"I'm sure I don't need to go over the details of how she came to this," he said. "But Sherry is now without a spleen, has a broken arm and two broken legs, and gone through two surgeries of more than three hours to repair internal damage, along with many other problems related to this horrific assault. But she has fought hard through it all. This is why the senior class came to me and suggested to me the awarding of both the diploma and this very special award."

He then stepped off the platform and handed the microphone to Sherry.

Through her tear clouded eyes, she saw the audience on its feet applauding her. The roar of the applause was deafening. As the crowd settled back into its chairs and all grew quiet, it was time for her to speak. But she could find no words. Part of her wanted to scold them for turning on her, and part of her was so grateful. She was afraid of which would come out of her mouth.

But she managed a quick "Thank you all," then the emotion came bursting out of her in a full-throated cry.

The receiving line for graduates was formed, and Sherry was wheeled to the end of it. Everyone who went through the line shook her hand and bent to kiss her. Several people told her they were sorry for anything negative they had said about her or done to her. It struck Sherry as ironic that it took something like her pain and agony to make people feel and express sorrow for their actions or words toward her. They judged her for something they knew nothing about.

Alone in Sherry's hospital room following the graduation ceremony, Barry and Sherry discussed their future. Barry was planning to go to college in the fall. Sherry had hoped to go with him, but that was so uncertain now.

"I'll wait a year until you can come with me," Barry told her.

Sherry shook her head so violently that she grimaced in pain.

"I'm not going to stop you from going at all," she said firmly.

The stitches were out of her lip and an ugly scar remained. But there was still a bit of pain when she spoke, especially when she spoke quickly, firmly, and in even moderately long stretches.

"But we had planned to go together," Barry said just as firmly.

"I know what we planned," she said. "But it can't be done now."

She smiled sweetly and reached up with her uncasted arm and lightly stroked his face.

"Don't give up all your dreams just for me," she added. "Go ahead with your dreams. I will catch up."

"But I want to share my dreams with you," Barry protested.

"And you will," Sherry said, taking his hand in hers. "You will share your dreams with me, and I will share mine with you." She looked deeply into his eyes. "But we can't let each other pull either of us back," she said.

Barry shook his head.

"Dammit! You're going in September," she almost yelled it, sending pinpricks of pain across her scarred lip.

Barry was taken aback by her outburst. Such forcefulness from her he had never seen before.

"And what if I don't go?" he asked, looking away from her.

"If that is the case, I don't ever want to see you again."

Her answer surprised and shocked him, and he turned to face her. She noticed the fear in his look.

"Do you really mean that?" he asked hesitantly.

"Yes, I do."

"You're going to make me do the right thing even if it kills me, aren't you?" he asked, with a little twinkle in his eye she couldn't help but notice. A big grin broke across her face.

"You better believe it," she responded.

He stood up from the chair and leaned over to give her the tightest hug he could.

"Who knows, I may be well enough to go with you anyway," she said. "There is a lot of time before September."

Chapter 9

The summer came too quickly for Sherry. Her recovery was slow. It wasn't until late June that she was released from the hospital.

The cast had been removed from her arm, but there were still a few weeks to go before the leg casts were removed. There was still danger of infection, especially if any foreign substances had not been removed before the casts were applied. She remained confined to a wheelchair for another month.

It was at this time that detectives from the Skamania County Sheriff's Department made an appointment to talk to her. They had done some preliminary interviews in between her surgeries, but because of her condition, they had been brief and provided only the basic details of her abduction and the attack in the clearing.

Now that she was stronger, detectives wanted to review what they had gathered and try to get more details.

Sergeants Dave Whisnofski and Stephen Pyle sat at the Dykes' kitchen table across from Sherry. Her parents sat at either end. The detectives had Sherry review the events starting with her walk home from the store up to the last thing she remembered, which was realizing she was at the highway. They had her go through it three times, with more details surfacing with each repetition.

Whisnofski and Pyle seemed satisfied with what they had so far.

"So how did you know it was Ted Brennen?" Pyle asked.

"I recognized his voice," Sherry answered.

"How long has it been since you've seen him, heard his voice?" Pyle asked.

"A little over a year," Sherry responded. "Just before we moved here."

"Was that right after he forced himself on you there?" Whisnofski asked.

Though the detective described the rape in gentler terms, the mention of the incident in the Mustang made Sherry shiver in revulsion. She put her head in her hands. Her mother went to her side and wrapped her arm around her.

"Do we really have to relive that again?" Bob asked angrily.

"It is important to be able to establish her ability to recognize his voice," Pyle said. "A year is a long time."

Bob started to protest, but Sherry held up her hand to stop him.

"It's okay, Dad," she said then turned to the detectives. "I will never forget that voice," she said firmly. "I have absolutely no doubt it was him."

The two detectives looked at each other then back at Sherry.

"Okay, we'll accept that," Whisnofski said.

"About what happened to you in Wyoming," Pyle said. "You mentioned you had been dating him before you had sex with him…"

"She was raped, Detective," Bob said angrily.

"How long were you dating before the event?" he asked, making no indication he had heard Bob's comment but softening his description of the encounter between Sherry and Ted.

"About a month," Sherry said.

"During your dating, had there been any other sexual encounters?" Pyle asked.

Bob became more frustrated, and the officers both took mental note.

"No," Sherry said. "He tried a couple of times, but when I said no, he didn't push it."

"What made that last time different?" Whisnofski asked.

"I don't know," Sherry said.

"Were you wearing anything different, more revealing than you had before?" Pyle asked.

Bob slammed his fist on the table. The suddenness of it startled Sherry and Katrina, but the two detectives sat motionless and expressionless.

"So now you're trying to make it my daughter's fault that she was raped!" Bob hollered.

"Please calm down, Mr. Dyke," Whisnofski said, keeping his eyes fixed on Sherry, trying to gauge her reactions.

"Bullshit!" he yelled. His wife and daughter were beginning to see a side of him they had not seen before—angry and demonstrative. It was the first time Sherry had heard her father swear. "You guys aren't doing anything but trying to deflect the blame for all of this on my daughter."

"That is not what we are doing," Pyle said. "We're trying to cover all the angles that will come up if this goes to a trial."

"What do you mean 'if' this goes to trial?" Bob was close to screaming now. "It better make it to trial and with the right outcome."

Whisnofski stood and beckoned his partner to do the same. He gave Bob a steely-eyed look.

"Or what?" he asked.

"Or I may just have to take care of this situation myself," Bob said. "I should have done it before, and we wouldn't be in this situation now."

Whisnofski got almost nose to nose with Bob.

"It might be best if you rethought that statement," he said.

The two men stood staring at each other for a few seconds. Then Bob seemed to have calmed down a bit. He glanced at the officer's badge then down at the gun at his hip. A look past him at his partner was strong reinforcement. Bob relaxed his posture.

"Yes, sir," he said softly. "I agree, and I apologize."

"We get it, Mr. Dyke," Pyle said. "You're a father, and you want to protect your daughter. But you need to let us do our job."

Katrina finally spoke. "Maybe we should take a break in this, and maybe you can come back tomorrow to continue," she said with a calmness that surprised everyone in the room, including Sherry.

"I agree," Whisnofski said, still with his eyes locked on Bob.

Whisnofski and Pyle had a problem with the Sherry Dyke case. In fact, it wasn't just one problem; it was several.

To start with, as law enforcement officers, they were required to enter every case with an open mind, no biases. To ensure a fair investigation, they were supposed to suspect everyone and trust no one.

Their first problem was, they were deputy sheriffs in a rural county in a low population area of the state. The people they dealt with on the job—either victim or suspect—were people they knew. Sometimes they were neighbors, even close friends.

How can you treat everyone as a suspect and trust none of your neighbors and friends?

That built in another problem. If a suspect, or even a person of interest, was from outside the county, how could they be trusted? You knew nothing about them to start with, and anything you did know came after painstaking hard investigation.

The suspect in this case was from outside the county. He hadn't been in-county very long, no more than six months, from what their preliminary investigation had turned up. He had no family in the area and had survived by doing odd jobs, none of which were on the Washington side of the river. He confined his employment to the Oregon side, and he did not stay long in any one job.

This suspect had not helped himself any. When sheriff's deputies went to his Home Valley rooming house to question him as a person of interest, he bolted as soon as Sherry's name was mentioned. The ensuing chase down State Highway 14 to the Bridge of the Gods ended only when Ted crashed his car when he was boxed in.

The end of that chase also presented another problem—Barry's involvement and actions when he got to the crash site. It wasn't so much the one-punch, one-kick assault but the fact he told Ted, "I'd love to kill you." Never mind that he followed that with saying it was better to turn him over to the legal system. The threat combined with the assault could be used to paint Ted as an innocent victim.

A problem, but the other side of the coin of Barry's actions was Ted's once he was in custody. He was arrogant, belligerent, and aggressive with the officers on the way to the station for initial questioning. Once they had him in the interrogation room, officers barely had settled into their seats across the table from him when he lawyered up.

Other problems cropped up when deputies interviewed members of the Dyke family. Whisnofski and Pyle had driven to the Puget Sound Naval Shipyard to talk to Terry. He was on base assisting in the overhaul of the USS *Enterprise*, the ship to which he had been assigned.

During their conversation, it was clear the Dyke family was not at all fond of Ted.

"I hear you have Ted Brennen in jail for raping and beating my sister," Terry said when the introductions and small talk was completed.

Pyle looked at his partner before responding. "Well, Mr. Brennen is in custody, but he has not been charged with anything connected to your sister at this time," he responded.

"So when will that happen?" Terry asked.

"We're not here to discuss that," Whisnofski shot back firmly. "We have some questions for you."

Terry sat up stiffly in his chair. Being a US Navy sailor and still a seaman first class, he responded to an authoritative tone. But there was also some irritation building within him.

"Tell me about any connection between your family and Mr. Brennen," Whisnofski said.

Terry hesitated. He did not know how much his family had told the police about their past in Wyoming and why they had made the move to Washington. It was likely that these officers already knew the details, but he did not want to be the one to spill the beans if they had not.

"Sherry dated him briefly, but she broke it off after he mistreated her," Terry said.

"How did he mistreat her?" Pyle asked.

"I think those details should come from my parents," Terry answered.

"We have talked with them and plan to again," Pyle said. "But they are a little preoccupied right now with your sister's recovery. So it would be helpful if you could enlighten us."

"I still believe those details should come from them," Terry was steadfast. "All I will tell you is, he really mistreated her in a way that should have been prosecuted."

Pyle and Whisnofski looked at each other in frustration then back to Terry.

"So you think he found a way to get out of a legal spot?" Whisnofski asked.

"You can say that," Terry responded. Then showing more emotion than he had so far in the interview, he leaned forward and added, "But I'll tell you this. If he doesn't get what's coming to him this time, justice will catch up to him."

"I'd be careful about making threats, Seaman," Whisnofski commanded.

"Not making threats, sir," Terry said, dipping the word *sir* in bitter sarcasm. "Just saying it the way it is."

The two deputies left the Puget Sound Naval Shipyard feeling a little uneasy. That didn't change much after they talked to Ralph.

"Whatever it takes, whoever did this to my sister will pay," he had said during the interview back in Carson.

And then there was Bob's outburst the day before when they were finally questioning Sherry in-depth. All those things combined made it clear there was some hostility between the Dyke family and Ted. It was understandable, considering what took place north of Carson. But it certainly seemed to go deeper than that.

When Whisnofski and Pyle returned to the Dyke home for the second interview with Sherry, her father excused himself and left the house. Katrina and Sherry sat in the living room with the detectives this time. It provided a more casual setting and put Katrina and Sherry a little more at ease.

"I want to apologize for yesterday," Katrina said. "Bob is never like that. He's very calm and quiet. But all this is really getting to him."

"And how are you doing?" Pyle asked.

Katrina sighed heavily and paused for a moment before answering.

"Oh, I'm angry," she said. "But there is not a lot I can do but let you gentlemen and the rest of the legal system do your jobs."

"What if the system provides a resolution you do not agree with?" Whisnofski asked.

Again, Katrina sighed and paused. "Then we'll just have to cross that bridge when we come to it."

The detectives glanced at each other, then Pyle said, "Fair enough."

They both opened their small notebooks and poised their pens as they turned their attention to Sherry.

"We know this is difficult for you, but we need to go over some things from Wyoming and the incident here," Whisnofski told her apologetically.

Sherry nodded her understanding. She believed she was ready. She then explained, in specific detail, what happened in Ted's car the night of the Wyoming assault. In her first telling of it to her parents the day after, she had left out some of the explicit details, so Katrina was a little taken aback at times. But she fought to keep her composure. That was not lost on Pyle, whose task in the interview was to observe the mother for her reactions.

When Sherry sheepishly told them about getting the abortion, Whisnofski spoke up.

"Is there any way that he could have gotten the idea that you consented to sex?"

A painful whimper escaped Katrina's mouth before she could stop it. Sherry, with her wheelchair right next to her mother's chair, took Katrina's hand and squeezed it lightly.

"I told him more than once that I did not want to," Sherry said. She sat straight and attentive, but a tear began to form in her eye. "Then he hit me. I tried to push him off me, and he hit me again."

"Is that when he penetrated you?" Whisnofski asked.

It was fainter this time, but Katrina whimpered again.

"Yes," Sherry choked out.

"Now to the latest incident, you say you were taken from the street as you were walking home," Whisnofski said. "Did you see anything at all before they grabbed you?"

"No, someone from behind put their hand over my mouth and grabbed me around the waist with his other hand," she explained. "Then someone else put a blindfold on me."

Whisnofski penned some notes before speaking again.

"Then you were put in a vehicle," he said. "Was it a car or a truck?"

"It was a car," she answered.

"If you were blindfolded, how do you know?" the detective asked.

"Because it was lower to the ground than a truck," Sherry answered. "And it had four doors."

"Crew cab trucks have four doors," Whisnofski said without looking up from his notes.

"But they are higher off the ground," Sherry answered with conviction.

"The first time you spoke to us, you said they didn't put the blindfold on until you were in the car," Pyle said.

Sherry thought for a moment. The entire incident seemed so clear in her mind. But now she was uncertain. If she could not remember this detail correctly, what else might she have gotten wrong?

"I suppose it could have been done in the car, and maybe that is why I am sure the vehicle was a car," she said. "I must have seen it before they got the blindfold on me."

Both deputies made notes on their pads.

"Which way did they drive?" Pyle asked."

"They went north," Sherry said. Then she added as he started to ask another question, "I know because I heard the tires on the bridge north of town."

Now she wanted to provide every little detail she could remember in hopes that it convinced them she was telling the truth.

"How far did they drive after the bridge?" Whisnofski asked.

"Almost right after they got off the bridge, they turned right and were on a dirt road," she answered.

"How do you know they turned right?" the detective asked.

"Because of the motion of the car," Sherry said. "They were going kind of fast, and I got thrown to the side."

"How long did they drive on the dirt road?" Whisnofski asked.

"I don't know," Sherry said. "Maybe as long as they had driven since kidnapping me and making the turn on the dirt road."

"What happened when they stopped?" Whisnofski asked.

Sherry then took them through the entire rape and beating without interruption, again in vivid detail. Katrina fought to hold back her tears, having to get up and go into the kitchen twice during the telling to let the cry out then compose herself before returning.

Both times Sherry did not pause in her testimony to the detectives. She seemed to be on autopilot through this part of the interview. She was intent on remembering every detail but trying to distance herself from them.

When she got to the point where she lost total consciousness at the highway, she stopped talking, totally worn out mentally and physically. The detectives could see that but had a few more questions to ask.

"Just a few more questions, Sherry," Whisnofski said, with the first hint of empathy in his voice since the interview started the day before.

"So there were three people in total," he said. "Is there anything about the other two besides Ted that you can remember at all?"

She thought for a moment. "No, I was blindfolded right away, and I didn't take it off until I knew they were gone."

"The one who covered your mouth, that seems to be the only time there was skin-to-skin contact between you and the other two guys," Whisnofski said, and Sherry nodded after rolling the incident over in her mind again.

"When they were holding my arms, it was over my shirt sleeves," she explained. "The sleeves were down to about my elbows."

"Were you able to bend your arms at the elbows?" Whisnofski asked.

Sherry took a moment to recall again. If her hands and arms had some freedom of movement, had she tried to fight off her attackers?

"I don't remember for sure," she said. "They were squeezing my arms so tight and pulling them back so hard that it hurt my shoulders."

More notes were scribbled in the books.

"Was there anything about the hand over your mouth you can describe?" Whisnofski asked.

"It was rough, like when you work without gloves," Sherry said. "And it had a wood smell, kind of like my dad when he comes home from the mill."

"Did you hear their voices?" Whisnofski asked.

"No, they didn't say a word the whole time," Sherry answered. "And Ted never spoke directly to them."

Whisnofski looked at his partner, silently asking, "Do you have any other questions?" Pyle shook his head and closed his notebook, and Whisnofski followed suit. They both stood almost simultaneously.

"I think we have all that we need for now," Whisnofski said. "But we may want to talk to you again as things develop."

Sherry nodded weakly, and Katrina squeezed her hand before standing up.

"I'll walk you both out," the mother said.

The officers nodded and went outside, Katrina close behind. She followed them all the way out to their cruiser.

"What happens now?" she asked.

"We will go over all that we have gathered with the county attorney, and he will decide whether charges will be filed," Pyle explained.

"What are the possibilities of that?" Katrina asked.

Both detectives sighed.

"It is hard to say, Mrs. Dyke," Whisnofski answered. "We can't really talk about the case since it is an ongoing investigation."

Katrina was not satisfied with the answer but knew there was very little information she was going to get at this point.

"So will Ted stay in jail? Is my daughter safe?" Katrina asked.

"By law, he should have had a bail hearing already," Pyle explained. "But because he ran from the police and the length of your daughter's recovery, the county attorney was able to convince the judge he is a flight risk, and Sherry's additional surgeries kept us from talking to her in-depth."

"But now that we have talked to her, we're going to need to take our information to the prosecutor within the week, but he is still in jail on the charges stemming from his attempt to run after deputies went to talk to him," Whisnofski said. "So she is safe until that sentence has run its course. He will be released then."

"I understand," Katrina said. "I don't like it, but I understand."

The detectives looked at each other uneasily.

"I don't blame you for not liking it," Pyle said. "We'll stay in touch."

* * *

With his sentence completed, Ted was processed out of the county jail system. He was feeling cocky. The sixty days had passed fairly quickly, and now he would be free to resume his life. Just what he would do with it was not yet decided. But one thing he was sure of was, he was going to put as much distance between himself and the Columbia Gorge as he could.

He had had enough of his obsession with Sherry Dyke.

She's not worth all this, he thought as he was led down the hallway to the jail exit.

Not that Ted Brennen was any stranger to trouble in his life. He had been able to skirt any serious consequences from his past actions. He was just now ending his first taste of jail time, and it left a sour taste in his mouth. He was determined to do whatever it took to avoid it in the future.

As the detention officers opened the exit door, Ted saw standing just a few feet away county deputies Pyle and Whisnofski. He recognized them from his earlier questioning by them following the highway chase that ended on the Bridge of the Gods. He knew in an instant his plans to avoid any more time in jail was not going to come to fruition.

Whisnofski stepped forward with a pair of handcuffs in his hand.

"Ted Brennen, you are under arrest for the rape and assault of Sherry Dyke," he said.

Ted stood transfixed, unmoving, not quite ready to do what he knew was coming.

"Put your hands on your head," Whisnofski ordered, but Ted did not comply.

"Okay then," Whisnofski said as he grabbed his left wrist and tried to bend it behind his back.

Ted tried to jerk his arm away and started to turn toward the deputy. But Pyle reached out and grabbed his right arm and twisted it behind his back, pushing up toward Ted's neck. Ted yelped in pain, and Whisnofski snapped one of the cuffs on his left wrist then secured the other on his right, tightening both as far as they would go.

"Now we'll add resisting arrest to the charges," Pyle said as the two deputies passed Ted off to the detention officers and followed them into the building.

* * *

The Skamania County Courthouse, situated on a small rise on West Vancouver Avenue, does not appear like a building constructed in 1949. It has a more modern, boxy look. But inside, a courtroom is a courtroom, and Sherry and her parents sat in the first row for spectators behind the prosecution tables.

The defense tables were on the opposite side, but no one sat in the first rows behind Ted and his court-appointed attorney. Ted stared straight ahead, not looking toward the Dykes and the various friends surrounding them. Barry sat next to Sherry, holding her hand.

All stood when the judge entered then sat down for the preliminaries of the arraignment. Then the real meat of the event began.

Bill Shaw was a veteran with the Skamania County Attorney's Office. In his ten years with the agency, he could count on one hand, with three fingers left, the number of cases he had lost. Standing six feet and two inches at two hundred and twenty-five pounds, he looked like he could play football, which he had for Eastern

Washington University. He looked like a giant compared to his five-foot, eight-inch opponent, who looked like he was just out of college, which, in fact, he was.

It was quite a mismatch.

It was Ted's first appearance in court on the new charges. During this arraignment, he was advised of the charges against him. Shaw read out rape, assault, and battery and attempted murder. He was very confident he could get a conviction on the first two, but the third was thrown in as a bargaining tool. He fully expected the case to go to trial, but he was ready to drop the attempted murder charge if that would get it there.

Following the reading of the charges, the judge asked if he understood them.

"I understand what they are accusing me of, but it's all bullshit," Ted responded defiantly. His attorney, public defender Keith Ryan, turned to give Ted a look of admonishment.

Judge Ronald Belfor banged his gavel on the Portland Buckaroos hockey puck he used as a gavel pad. The team had played in the Western Hockey League, but the circuit was about to cease operations.

"That will be quite enough of that language," he said. "You will show proper respect in this court, or I will find you in contempt."

Shaw smiled inwardly. He knew Judge Belfor ran a tight court and expected the best of decorum at all times. This could work in his favor later on.

"Do you accept your court-appointed attorney to represent you?" the judge asked.

"Since I can't afford one, the little sh—" Ted started but cut himself off when the judge raised his gavel. "The little guy will do."

"A simple yes or no will do, Mr. Brennen," Judge Belfor said as he eased the gavel down on the hockey puck.

"Is there anything else to come before this court in this matter at this time?" the judge asked. Both attorneys said there was none.

"Therefore, the next proceeding in this manner will be a bail hearing," the judge informed them. "The court calendar is quite full and in flux right now, so I will inform you of the date and time."

With that, the proceedings for Ted's case were completed for that day.

*　*　*

The time had come for Ted's bail hearing. With Sherry now out of the hospital, the entire Dyke family who had missed the first court appearance was in attendance.

"Your Honor, we ask that no bail be set for this defendant," Shaw said from his seat at the table. "He has demonstrated that he is a flight risk. He bolted when officers went to question him, and he led a high-speed chase down State Route 14 and would have gotten away had it not been for an Oregon State Police roadblock on the Bridge of the Gods."

He closed the folder in front of him, paused for a moment, then turned to look at Sherry sitting in her wheelchair, her legs still in casts that were prominently displayed as she had worn a midthigh skirt, as instructed by Shaw.

He turned back to face the judge after only a few seconds.

"And the brutality of the attack Mr. Brennen rained down on upon the victim, Sherry Dyke, demonstrates that he is capable of heinous violence," he said.

"I object!" Keith Ryan shouted, standing up from his chair. "It has not been established that my client participated in any attack on his client."

Before the judge could rule, Shaw bowed slightly at the waist toward Ryan then addressed the judge.

"My esteemed colleague is correct. I will rephrase," Shaw said with only the slightest hint of sarcasm. "The alleged brutal attack on Sherry Dyke indicates, if proven, the defendant is allegedly capable of heinous violence."

Shaw, still seated at the table, opened a second folder.

"But the flight risk is well-documented," he said. He handed copies of the police reports about the chase to his assistant, who took them to the judge. He then called each officer involved in the chase to the stand to testify to the events.

When they had all spoken, Shaw said his presentation was complete. The judge turned to Ryan. He stood to make his case.

"My client was new to this community," he said. "He panicked. He knows what he did by trying to escape the questioning was wrong and has signed an affidavit that he will remain in Skamania County until this matter is resolved."

Ryan walked to the judge's bench to hand him the affidavit. He had no assistant.

"We have also arranged for him to return to his most recent job at the sawmill," Ryan added when back at his table.

After a few moments of silence, Judge Ronald Belfor held out his hands in an anticipatory gesture.

"Do you have any more to provide the court?" he asked.

Ryan shook his head, and Judge Belfor looked to Shaw.

"We have reason to believe Mr. Brennen may have come to Washington, in part, to stalk Sherry Dyke and as a means to get away from some legal trouble in Wyoming," he said.

Ryan again jumped to his feet. "I object!" he shouted. "That is pure inuendo! It is not supported by any evidence."

"Calm down, Mr. Ryan," Judge Belfor said. "I know what it is."

While Ronald Belfor was new to the bench in Skamania County, having been elected only two years previously, as a defense attorney in the county for three years prior, he had numerous occasions to see Shaw's tactics in the courtroom.

"Mr. Shaw, do you have anything to substantiate your beliefs in this regard?" the judge asked.

"Your Honor, we are waiting for documentation from the Fremont County Sheriff's Office in Wyoming, but we are informed by deputies there that there have been incidents there that indicate just that," Shaw answered casually.

"I will consider any such documentation when I have it in my hands," Belfor said. "In the meantime, give me a few minutes to look over the documentation I do have."

The judge gathered the papers in front of him and adjourned to his chambers. Those in the courtroom sat back down to wait. They didn't have to wait more than ten minutes before the judge returned.

Once everyone was back in their seats, Judge Belfor arranged his paperwork, looked at each attorney in turn, then began to speak.

"After reading over the documents and conducting some research of my own, I have decided to allow bail for this defendant," he said.

Ted pumped his fist in triumph, and Ryan smiled. The Dykes and their friends gasped in surprise.

"What the hell!" Bob Dyke said angrily.

Judge Belfor looked in his direction and seemed about to say something to him, but Shaw, who had not reacted at all when the judge pronounced bail would be allowed, turned toward the Dykes and gave them a look that said, "It will be okay."

When Shaw turned back to look at the bench, Judge Belfor announced, "Bail is set at seven hundred-fifty thousand dollars."

Ryan's jaw dropped to the floor, and Ted's face went white as a sheet.

Chapter 10

In late July, the casts Sherry lugged around were removed, and she was able to leave the wheelchair. But she had to use braces to make her legs stable until she got used to using them again. She went to the clinic in Stevenson for daily physical therapy to strengthen her legs and arm.

Sherry underwent two more operations to repair internal damage. After the leg casts were removed, the doctor discovered some infection in her left leg.

But with the constant support of her family, Barry, and the newfound and rejuvenated friends in town, she continued to fight through it.

All that had taken place before the bail hearing. And then Sherry faced something else painful in the worst summer of her life.

At the end of August, she stood on her own, without braces or support, although a bit wobbly, as Barry packed his car at his home in Stevenson to leave for college. Karen had driven her there and was helping Barry put things in his trunk. The back seat was also packed full.

The additional surgeries and infection made it impossible for Sherry to go with him. It was gut-wrenching for them both. And to add to Sherry's anguish, Karen would soon be gone as well, off to the University of Puget Sound near Seattle to begin her college studies.

When the packing was complete, Barry held Sherry tight, not wanting to let go. His reassuring words could not stop her tears.

"I love you, Sherry," he said to her. "I'll be back. Whatever breaks I get and whenever I need to be here for any legal things I have to be part of, I'll be here."

"I wish you could be here through the whole thing," she said. "I'm scared."

Barry lifted her chin, so she was looking him right in the eyes.

"I know you're scared. But don't be," he said in a tone that held her rapt attention. "There is nothing that creep can do to you now. We're going to see to it that his ass rots in prison for what he did to you."

Anger was in his voice, as it always was when he was forced to talk about Ted. His pretrial hearing was scheduled for the county courthouse in two weeks. His lawyer had tried to get it moved to Vancouver due to the sentiment against him, and rising, in Carson and Stevenson. Ryan also hinted that if Ted was held over for trial, he would make the motion again as he claimed there could never be an unbiased jury in Skamania County. But the judge ruled against him and kept the pretrial hearing in Stevenson.

"Always come back to me," Sherry pleaded with tears in her soft brown eyes as Barry tore himself away to begin his drive to La Grande.

Barry couldn't take it any longer and broke down himself, hugging her tightly one last time. They wept together for long minutes that seemed like just seconds. Finally, he pulled back and gave her a long kiss. He climbed into his car and quickly drove away.

There was now nothing to stop the tears from pouring from Sherry's eyes and soul as his car disappeared down the road. Karen tried to console her, but there was nothing she could do.

* * *

Being back at the clearing where she was attacked gave Sherry the chills. Every so often, she had to choke back a gag reflex when she was forced to recall the events.

Shaw wanted to see if Sherry could remember anything more about the incident. He was hoping to find something that would positively identify Ted as the main attacker and give some idea who the other two were. He was a confident prosecutor—some might call it arrogant. But his thoroughness was critical to his career success so far.

They had started at the dirt road off the highway just north of the Wind River Canyon bridge where Sherry was found that morning. Shaw, the two sheriff's deputies, and Bob Dyke parked their cars along the highway shoulder. Bob and Katrina helped Sherry out of the car. She used crutches, and her parents stayed on either side to help her if needed.

The Dykes joined Shaw and the deputies, not Whisnofski and Pyle, at the head of the dirt road.

"I know this is difficult, especially because of your health," Shaw said apologetically, glancing at Sherry's legs. "But the information we could gather would really help in this case."

Sherry nodded. "I understand," she said.

"Anytime you need to stop and rest, just say so," Shaw said, holding up a small folding aluminum and plastic patio chair.

"Now as we walk up the road, I want everyone to stay to the side and as much in the grass as you can," he explained.

Shaw did not want anything in the dirt road disturbed. Deputies had taken plaster casts of tire tracks at the head of the road the day Sherry was found. But there had been traffic up and down the road in the months since. Still, Shaw did not want to disturb the road in case they saw something of significance.

"As we go up the road, I want you to tell me if there is anything you remember, no matter how insignificant you think it might be," he instructed Sherry. "Especially let me know if you recognize the clearing you were taken to."

Shaw had not been to the site, and he specifically requested deputies who had not been there either. He wanted Sherry to find the clearing on her own. He believed that not only would it help her recall details she might have forgotten but he could use the fact that she had found it without any help when the case went to trial. It might even be helpful in the pretrial hearing.

The going was slow as Sherry had trouble navigating with her crutches in the grass next to the road. She moved the crutches forward one at a time to test the solidity of the ground before moving forward with her feet then the other crutch. They had started at seven o'clock in the morning, so there was plenty of time.

"We'll take all day if we have to," Shaw had said after they had advanced thirty yards, and Sherry apologized for her pace.

After another forty-five minutes, one of the deputies held up his hand for the others to stop then carefully stepped to the center of the road and kneeled. There was a softball-sized rock embedded in the roadway with a brown stain across the top.

"Could be dried blood," Deputy Steve Cransky said.

He pulled a pocketknife out, opened a blade, and carefully dug the rock from the dirt. He slipped it in an evidence bag and sealed it then returned to the north side of the road. The group continued on.

Twice during the next thirty minutes, Sherry thought she recognized an opening in the trees on the south side of the road that could have led to a clearing. But when Deputy Cransky and Deputy Scott Detimore investigated, they found them too small to accommodate more than a vehicle.

The third time Sherry indicated a possible clearing, those accompanying her knew this was the place. Sherry had a pained look roll across her face, and she became wobbly on the crutches. Bob and Katrina reached out to support her.

They all saw a pathway into a stand of trees. It was a little more than two parallel worn spots in the grass, with the bare ground just wide enough to accommodate a vehicle tire. The deputies noticed a set of tire tracks coming off the dirt road and going onto the worn pathway. No one apparently had been on this pathway since Sherry was attacked as only one set of tire tracks clearly arched into and out of the pathway in both directions from the dirt road.

The tracks left in the dirt looked identical to the ones plaster casted where the dirt road met the highway.

"Whoever it was drove in from the west then backed out to go back the same way or drove past this point, backed in, then drove out to the west," Detimore said.

The group followed the pathway for about fifty feet where it opened into a larger clearing. Directly across was a firepit, and behind it was a small pile of rocks. Everyone looked to Sherry, who was in tears, nodding.

"This is where they attacked?" Shaw asked. "You are absolutely sure?"

Sherry continued to nod, only more forcefully.

The two deputies began to circle the clearing at its edges, looking inward. The entire clearing was covered with grass, but it was mostly matted down from multiple uses. In the center, leading from the worn pathway from the dirt road, there were two tracks very slightly less matted, but within them, four spots more matted down.

"That looks like someone drove in and stopped for a while," Detimore said.

Cransky carefully moved into the clearing. As he did with the tracks coming off the dirt road, he took a number of pictures of the matted areas with a Pentax K1000 single-lens reflex camera with a detachable flash.

Shaw went to Sherry and unfolded the patio chair and motioned for her to sit down. At first, she refused. But her mother insisted.

"You need to get off your feet and rest," she said firmly. Sherry complied but kept her attention focused on the clearing.

While she had been shocked and sick to her stomach when they entered the scene of the rape and attack, the more she sat in that clearing and remembered the events, the more those feelings left her. Instead, she was beginning to be filled with rage at what had been done to her.

Continuing their search of the clearing, the deputies found dried brown spots. There were three distinct splotches, and they formed a line between the rock pile and the clearing opening. They also found a larger concentration of rust-brown spots on several rocks near the center of the pile.

Clippings were taken from the grass and bagged, as were several rocks from the pile.

After these samples were taken, Shaw conferred with the deputies and went to the Dykes.

"The deputies believe we have gotten all we would get from the dirt road," he told Bob. "So you can go back and get your car to pick up Sherry."

Without hesitation, Bob took off.

"The deputies and I will stick around a bit to see if there is anything else to gather," Shaw told Katrina and Sherry.

He looked appreciatively at Sherry sitting in the patio chair.

"Thank you for having the courage to come back out here," he said. "What we found so far makes our case stronger."

For the first time that day, a small smile crept across Sherry's face.

* * *

Following her release from the hospital, Bob and Katrina moved Sherry to their ground-floor master bedroom. They also had Mary sleep there. She slept on a sturdy Army surplus cot Bob had purchased at the secondhand store. Sherry had to sleep alone so her casted legs and arms would not be jarred during the night.

When the casts were removed, the physical therapists gave the okay for her to return to her second-story bedroom. They said the exercise going up and down the stairs would be good extra therapy for Sherry's legs.

Bob installed stout handrails on both walls of the stairs for Sherry to use for support when going up or down. She also had two pairs of crutches, one for upstairs and another for downstairs and when she left the house.

Sherry and Karen sat side by side on Sherry's bed in her room. Karen had come to say goodbye to her friend as she was scheduled to begin the drive to Puget Sound that afternoon.

"I'm really going to miss you," Sherry said, knowing tears weren't far away but fighting to keep them in.

"I'll miss you too," Karen said. "But I'll come back on weekends sometimes and whenever you need me otherwise."

Sherry knew her friend could not drop everything at college and come streaking back to Carson every time she might need to talk or if she needed a hug. She did know that Karen would be back for a day or two when a trial was in session. Shaw had taken her deposition the day before and planned to call her as a witness.

But Sherry wished there was some way she could have her friend beside her or close at hand every day.

Karen seemed to understand what she was thinking.

"I could still put off my enrollment until next semester or even next year," Karen offered with conviction.

"Oh no, you will not," Sherry said firmly. "You are going to college."

Karen was a bit relieved. While she would have delayed in a second her departure as long as possible, she was eager to begin the next stage of her life. Like most teenagers in the small logging town, Karen wanted to get out and find a better occupation than retail or millwork.

"I will if you're sure you'll be all right," Karen said. "Barry's gone, and now I'll be gone. I want to be sure you're going to be okay."

Sherry put her hand on her friend's knee and gave her a reassuring pat then wrapped her arm around her neck and gave her a warm hug.

"I'll be fine," she said. "I've got my parents, my brother and sisters."

"Are you scared?" Karen asked.

"No," Sherry answered after a second's thought. "The therapy is hard, but I know I can handle it. And I'm feeling stronger a little bit each day."

"Well, I was talking about something else," Karen said. "Are you scared about Ted?"

Sherry was a bit puzzled.

"He's in jail," she responded. "He can't hurt me now."

"But what if he gets off?" Karen asked.

"I don't see how he could," Sherry said. She paused for a moment before going on. "And even if he did, I doubt he would try anything," she finally said. "He would probably leave this area."

"He doesn't sound like the type who would let things go," Karen said.

"You might be right," Sherry said. "But there are a lot of people around here who would make sure he couldn't come near me again."

Karen marveled at her friend's confidence. When she first met Sherry, she was shy and introverted. While she had seen that change in her friend in the past year, especially after she and Barry spent more time together, she still seemed a bit unsure of herself.

"What do you think will happen to him?" Karen asked.

Sherry took her arm from around Karen's neck and put her hand in her lap, grasping the other one. She was pensive for a moment, and Karen began to think she had somehow offended her with the question. She was about to retract the question when Sherry began to speak.

"I don't know," she said. "But I'll tell you what I'd like to happen to him."

Sherry's face took on a darker, more intense look. It gave Karen a bit of a fright.

"I would want him to know the suffering I went through," Sherry said, then she went on. "He would know how it is to have both your legs broken, an arm broken, to be beaten and kicked. He would know what it was like to be raped."

Sherry gripped her hands together tighter. Karen could see her fingers reddening each time she squeezed them together. It looked as if she were strangling an imaginary victim. The behavior heightened Karen's fright to see her friend in this way.

"He would be blindfolded when this is done to him, just like I was," Sherry went on. "And when it was done, he would get to see who had done it to him."

Karen shivered at the images Sherry's description produced.

Then Sherry's face lightened, and she looked more like herself.

"But that's something I could never do," Sherry said.

Karen was a bit surprised to realize she wasn't so sure that was true.

Chapter 11

Sherry stood in the front yard of her home waiting for her mother to join her. Part of her physical therapy was to walk as much as possible. She had decided to walk in the early mornings as far as she could and increase that each day. As she felt better, she would add other walks during the day.

This day, as she waited for Katrina, Sherry looked at Carson and its surroundings.

The sun was just breaking over the mountain to the east. Its rays painted a colorful picture as the leafy trees were beginning to show the yellows, reds, browns mixed with the summer green that remained. The pine trees were just beginning to show the first rust-colored needles. The light dew on the grass sparkled like the disco balls hanging from dance club ceilings.

There was a light breeze blowing up from the Columbia River less than a mile to the south. It put a chill in the air, foretelling the colder temperatures, and maybe even some snow, to come.

This early in the day, there was some activity as people began to head to work or school, but not so much that she could not hear the birds chirping and the breeze whistling through the trees in its whispered buzz. It was almost as if the birds were discussing their upcoming trip south for the winter and the wind was joining the conversation.

The panoramic natural masterpiece mesmerized Sherry. She loved the outdoors and the peace it provided. She was eager to get back into the woods around town. That was her greatest motivation to regain the strength in her limbs and rejuvenate her spirit.

So far, she was finding success.

Katrina came through the front door and, seeing her daughter admiring the scenery, stopped and watched for a few moments. She felt a lump work its way up her throat and felt a tear start rolling down her cheek. She could only imagine the pain Sherry felt, and continued to feel, both physical and emotional, since the attack. As much as she anguished for her oldest daughter, she also felt the anger building up inside her.

Ever since Sherry had identified Ted as her attacker, Katrina was filled with a sense of rage, and it intensified with each passing day. But she knew she had to keep a tight control on her feelings. Being a father, Bob was quick to action, as his outburst during the first talk with Deputies Whisnofski and Pyle had shown.

No, Katrina had to be the emotional rock for the family. But it was not an easy task.

Finally, Katrina stepped off the porch and slowly walked to Sherry's side. The daughter glanced at her mother and smiled. She noticed the dried tear track but said nothing.

"Are you ready?" Katrina asked.

Sherry took one last look around then nodded. The two women walked out into the street and headed north.

Sherry's pace was slow at first. She was a little unsteady on her feet. This was her first attempt at more than just short walks without her crutches. Each step was placed firmly on the ground and its security tested before she took the next step. Her mother was patient and stood ready to support her if she began to lose her balance.

"It's okay, Mom. I'm sure I've got it," Sherry said. "But thank you for being here for me."

"I will always be here for you," Katrina said, swallowing the lump back down her throat. "We all will be."

"I know," Sherry said. "I really appreciate you all."

They walked in silence for a short while, Sherry picking up the pace ever so slightly after advancing several steps, then a little more.

"I hadn't seen Karen around much in the last few days before she left for college," Katrina said. "You two were thick as thieves. What's going on?"

"I think I scared her a little bit," Sherry said sheepishly.

"How did you do that?" her mother asked.

"We were talking in my room the other day, and she asked me what I wanted to see happen to Ted," Sherry answered.

"Why would that scare her?" Katrina inquired.

"I told her I wanted him to feel exactly what I have felt," Sherry said. "I was pretty graphic about it, talking about wanting him to somehow feel what it was like to be raped and having his legs and arm broken."

"Not to mention all the other pain you've been through," Katrina said after a few seconds' thought.

Sherry stopped in her tracks and looked at her mother.

"What do you mean?" she asked.

Sherry's sudden stop took her mother by surprise, and she advanced a step before coming to a halt. She turned to face Sherry, took the few steps back toward her, and put her hands on her shoulders, as if what she were about to say might make Sherry unsteady on her feet.

"Sherry, you and I share wishes for that asshole," Katrina said.

Sherry did become a little unsteady from the shock, but it was not so much because of what her mother said but her use of the word asshole. It was very much unlike her.

"Oh my god, Mom," Sherry said. "I can't imagine you wishing anything bad on anyone."

"And I would never have expected it of myself," Katrina said as they resumed the walk. "But he did vile things to one of my children. That changed me in ways I could never have imagined."

Sherry let a small giggle escape her lips.

"That's for sure. Asshole? I've never heard you swear before," she said.

"It's not the first time, nor do I think it will be the last," Katrina said. "Your father and I have tried to raise you children by example, so we've worked very hard to stay away from language like that…and other things."

They walked in silence for a few moments. Then Katrina spoke again.

"And we want to keep raising you all by the best example," she said. "That is why my language and how I feel about what should happen to Ted needs to stay just between us."

"I understand," Sherry said.

She stopped in the street again, and her mother turned back to her.

"I think I've gone far enough for this walk," Sherry said. And they turned around and headed back toward the house.

There were two vehicles parked in front of the house when Sherry and Katrina approached. One was a Skamania County Sheriff's Office cruiser; the other a 1972 Lincoln Continental with a black hard top. Deputies Whisnofski and Pyle were in the cruiser, and Prosecutor Shaw was behind the wheel of the Continental.

All three exited their vehicles when they saw Sherry and Katrina coming. Mother and daughter saw that Bob was sitting on the porch.

"Hello, Sherry, Mrs. Dyke," Shaw said when they walked up. He extended his hand to both, then they shook hands with the deputies.

"We'd like to talk to you about the case," Shaw said.

Katrina bade them to come inside their home. Bob whispered something in her ear as they all passed. He quickly shook hands with the deputies and Shaw then walked to the backyard.

"We would like Bob to be included in this discussion," Shaw said as they entered the home.

"Because of his outburst the first time, he thinks it best that he not sit in," Katrina explained. "I can let him know what was discussed."

Sherry went to the kitchen table and sat down.

"She seems to be recovering well," Shaw said.

Katrina looked to her daughter with pride.

"She is strong and very determined," she said then waved the three men into the kitchen. "Would you like some coffee?" she asked.

Shaw and Pyle said they would, but Whisnofski said he preferred some water. The three men sat at the table. Once they had their drinks in front of them, Katrina took a seat.

Shaw looked to the deputies, indicating they had the floor.

"The tire impressions we made at the clearing did not match Ted's Mustang," Pyle said. "And all the blood we found there was Sherry's."

"We also went over Sherry's clothing very carefully," Whisnofski picked up the narration without hesitation. "On the right sleeve of her shirt, we found one thumbprint, and we found a partial print, not sure which finger, on the left sleeve."

He paused for a few seconds to let the women take in those details.

"Neither of those prints matched Mr. Brennen," Whisnofski finally said. The disappointment was clear on both Sherry's and Katrina's faces.

"That was all you found, just two fingerprints?" Katrina asked.

"According to Sherry, Mr. Brennen only touched the front of her shirt and bra and the front of her pants and panties," Pyle explained. "When she crawled out to the road, those areas collected so much dust and dirt that if there had been any prints to find, they were obliterated."

"What about the two prints you did get?" Sherry asked. "Who do they belong to?"

"Unfortunately, we don't know," Pyle said. "We have already begun to fingerprint as many men in the area as we can. Based on Sherry's assertion that the three men smelled like her dad when he comes home from the mill, we have already started collecting fingerprints from men who work at all the sawmills in the area."

At this point, Shaw took over the conversation.

"The problem is, that is going to take time, more time than we have," he said. "If anything is found, it won't be in time for next week's pretrial hearing."

"What does that mean?" Katrina asked.

GORGE JUSTICE

Shaw sighed heavily. It made Katrina and Sherry uneasy.

"It would really be helpful to us to know who those fingerprints belong to," Shaw said. "If we could identify them, they might roll over on Mr. Brennen."

"What do you mean by roll over?" Sherry asked.

"I mean they would identify him and confirm he was the one who attacked you," Shaw explained. He spoke to Sherry in a very patient manner, not condescending or highbrow. His approach was meant to give her reason to trust him, and it worked.

"Since you can't talk to those guys, does that mean he won't go to trial?" Katrina asked. She would not use his name, referring to him only when she had to.

Again, the heavy sigh from Shaw put her and Sherry ill at ease.

"I'm not going to tell you this is a slam dunk. It may not even be a 'Rip City,'" Shaw said, referring to the broadcasting catchphrase popularized by Portland Trailblazers broadcaster Bill Schonely. Katrina and Sherry were familiar with the phrase, so they understood Shaw's intent in using it.

"Everything we have been able to recover, Sherry's description, and the doctor's reports make it clear there was an attack and rape," Shaw said, noticing the pained looks on the women's faces when he used the word *rape*. "But the only thing we have connecting Mr. Brennen to the crime is Sherry's claim that it was his voice."

"What, you don't believe her?" Katrina said, her anger starting to rise.

Shaw shook his head vigorously and waved his right hand back and forth.

"That's not it at all. I do believe her," Shaw said. "I believe wholeheartedly that she knows exactly who it was that attacked her." This time, he made sure not to use the word *rape*. "But I also know that the defense attorney will do his best to tear that apart in court. And since there is no other physical evidence to connect Mr. Brennen to the scene, he might be successful in convincing the judge there is not enough evidence to hold him over to trial."

Katrina and Sherry looked at each other, both feeling a little less sure of the outcome of this case than they had been earlier that day.

"So what more do you need?" Katrina asked.

"Pretty much anything else you can remember," Shaw said directly to Sherry.

Everyone around the table fell silent for a few moments. Sherry closed her eyes and thought back over the entire incident, trying to pull as much from her memory as she could. But she could think of nothing else that could put Ted at the scene of the crime.

"At any time were you able to see anything, maybe even a small slit of vision from that blindfold?" Pyle asked. "Tell me about that blindfold. Was it a handkerchief, a towel?"

Sherry thought deeply.

"It was a bandana, I think," she responded.

"What color?" the deputy asked.

"I think it was red, with those white and black patterns on it," she said.

"Like plaid?" Pyle asked.

"No, the white patterns were like kind of a curly Q with some black trim," Sherry said.

Katrina's head shot up, and she quickly got out of her seat and went to a drawer and pulled out just such a cloth.

"Like this?" she asked her daughter.

Sherry nodded.

"How did you know what it looked like?" Whisnofski asked.

"I remember a flash of red when they first put it on, then when they stopped in the clearing and opened the door, the inside light came on, and I saw the pattern," Sherry explained.

"Did they take it off of you before they left?" Shaw asked.

Sherry shook her head. "I took it off after they left," she said.

"Did you take it with you?" Shaw asked.

"I don't think so," Sherry said. "I think I just dropped it right after I took it off."

Shaw looked at the deputies, asking the question with his eyes.

"They did not find anything like that at the clearing," Pyle said. "But Steve and I will go back out there and check things over again."

"That could be significant," Shaw said. "If we can establish that Mr. Brennen owns these types of bandannas, that would help."

"How so?" Katrina asked.

"Usually, these are sold in sets, so if he has one, there's a good chance he would have others," Shaw answered.

Suddenly, Sherry's eyes popped open as wide as silver dollars. All eyes turned to her.

"I remember something," she said excitedly. "When he pulled his pants down, I could see a little bit at the bottom of the blindfold. He had red bikini underwear on."

As he had with her other comments, Whisnofski wrote that in his notebook.

"And there is something else," Sherry said, blushing a little. "He was not circumcised."

Katrina looked at her daughter, surprised. "How did you know that?" she asked.

The men at the table became a little uncomfortable. They had all dealt with numerous sex crimes in the past. Whenever they dealt with teenagers describing sex acts in front of their parents, it was always uncomfortable. Most times, embarrassing secrets came out of it.

"Mom, I have seen pictures of penises, circumcised and not, in the sex education books," Sherry said, a little annoyed. "Besides, I have had that disgusting thing inside me before."

Now it was Katrina's turn to blush.

"Well, those things could be helpful," Shaw said, shooting glances at the deputies. They knew what to do.

Sherry stayed in the house when Katrina walked Shaw and the deputies to their cars.

"We have tried to raise our kids right, to keep them away from such things," she said. Shaw knew she was talking about premarital sex. He had heard it from numerous parents over the years.

"Katrina, I am certain that you and your husband have done a great job of raising your kids," Shaw said to her, as the deputies drove off to reexamine the clearing. "From everything I've heard, Sherry's introduction to sex was not something she sought out. But I also see a young woman who is wise beyond her years. That is something you and Bob should be very proud of."

Katrina felt a little relief.

"Thank you," she said. "But it's hard to see that when you're in the middle of something like this."

"I understand," Shaw said and extended his hand. But Katrina did not accept it.

"I do wonder though why you refer to Ted as Mr. Brennen," she said. "The way we were raised and how we raised our kids is that *Mr.* and *Mrs.* are terms of respect. Ted Brennen deserves no respect from anyone."

Shaw retracted his hand and looked Katrina firmly in the eyes.

"That is true, in the normal course of life," he said. "But in the courtroom, it is a little different. I will never refer to him by his first name because that humanizes him, makes him seem like a person. I won't do that."

He paused a moment before going on.

"On the other hand, I will always refer to Sherry by her first name, and I will never call her the victim," he said. "I want the judge, and eventually a jury, to see her as the person in this tragedy."

Katrina smiled and stuck out her hand. Shaw took it warmly and shook it.

Chapter 12

Barry guided his Grand Prix along State Route 14 heading east, retracing his steps of the late evening before. It was Friday, and he and Sherry were headed to Hood River, Oregon. They had a full day planned.

Ted's pretrial hearing was scheduled for the following Monday. Barry came home from La Grande Thursday night with the idea that he was going to give Sherry a day of fun to try and keep her mind off what was coming. Bob and Katrina were pleased with the plan and offered to fund the trip. But Barry politely refused. He wanted to do this for Sherry himself.

Barry's plan for the day was breakfast in The Dalles's novelty shops; a movie; then back to Carson, with a possible stop in Hood River for more shopping. Once back in Carson, they would join their families for a dinner at the Dykes' house.

The twenty-mile drive from Carson to the Hood River Bridge went quickly as the couple, who hadn't seen each other in weeks, jabbered back and forth without hesitation, catching up. Barry did most of the talking, describing life on the Eastern Oregon State College campus and how things were going with his classes.

Barry's classes load featured all basic courses in his first year to get as many of the requirements out of the way as quickly as possible before he began taking the courses specific to his major.

He had also gotten a part-time job as the small four-year college's sports information director. His duties were writing press releases and keeping and compiling statistics for the school's fall sports teams. Since the cross-country and volleyball teams took care of their own stats, the only ones he took himself, at least at home games, was the football team's. Since the Mounties were on the road the next day at Southern Oregon State College, he had a Saturday off. That was what allowed him to come home and be with Sherry.

He had also arranged to miss classes Monday to attend the hearing.

When Barry turned onto the Hood River Bridge, the conversation stopped as they crossed the river. The sound of the rubber tires on the steel grid of the road base was like running over a four-thousand-foot cattle guard. The resulting noise required shouting. They were willing to be quiet for ten minutes. But once they were on Interstate 80 headed east, the jabbering continued.

Breakfast at Cousins was hearty and filling. The restaurant, in addition to having a distinctly country, family-friendly atmosphere, served large portions. Barry's country fried steak and eggs with mashed potatoes and country gray was enough to keep him fed all day, even though he left a few scraps on his plate. Sherry had a stack of strawberry pancakes that she could not finish.

They walked off some of the heavy meal as they visited three shops. But none had anything they were particularly interested in buying. When they exited the last shop, it was showtime.

While they watched *The Land That Time Forgot*, a holdover from the previous week's releases, they munched on a shared large bag of popcorn and slurped a shared large soda. They both found the movie a little hokey and far-fetched, but it was the only one of the selections they were interested in seeing.

By the time the movie ended, there was not enough time to stop and shop in Hood River. Besides, neither of them were interested. They wanted to get home for the family get-together.

Barry had been concerned about the long day out for Sherry. He was afraid all the activity might be too tiring for her. But he underestimated Sherry's rehab work and her resolve. She had been pushing herself since he went to college, and she was in pretty good shape. She still had some work to do to get back to 100 percent, but she was well on her way.

As they turned off State Route 14 onto the Wind River Highway into Carson, they were eager to get to Sherry's house and the good times they anticipated with the two families.

Barry and Sherry walked into the Dyke house and were submerged into a very dark mood.

Barry's parents, Doug and Susan, were sitting on the couch. Katrina, Mary, and Kim were in the kitchen preparing the meal. Barry sat down on a chair in the living room.

"What's wrong?" Sherry asked Katrina.

"Your brother got suspended from school," her mother answered.

"But it wasn't his fault," Mary said from across the room. Katrina held her hand out to silence her daughter.

"He should have had better control of himself," Katrina said sternly.

"Where is he?" Sherry asked.

"He is upstairs talking to your father," Katrina answered. "Let them be," she added when Sherry started to head upstairs.

"How long is he suspended? What happened?" Sherry asked.

"Two weeks," Katrina said. She had never stopped what she was doing and never looked up even when she shushed Mary.

Sherry went into the living room and motioned for Barry to follow her outside. They settled into the front porch swing.

"What did your mom say?" Barry asked. He had been busy quizzing his parents and did not hear the kitchen conversation.

"Ralph got suspended from school for two weeks," she responded.

"What happened?" he asked.

"Mom didn't say," Sherry said. "What did your parents say?"

"They didn't say anything about it," Barry answered. "I guess they hadn't heard or didn't want to say anything."

They sat in silence for a few minutes. Suddenly, Sherry took Barry's hand in hers and looked him in the eye.

"Thank you so much for coming home this weekend," she said lovingly. "And thank you for today. I know it was meant to give me a good day before court on Monday."

Barry squeezed her hand and lifted it to kiss the back of it.

* * *

Ralph sat on the edge of his bed facing his father sitting on a stool. The son was telling the father about the events that had led to his suspension from Stevenson High School.

It was Ralph's first year at the high school, and so far, things had gone well. Sherry had graduated there the previous June, despite her devastating injuries after the attack, and Mary was in her second year at the school. Because of that and the goodwill the Dyke family had enjoyed since Sherry's incident, Ralph was becoming popular.

He had gone out for football and was on the junior varsity team. Being a bit big for his age, at six feet and a little over two hundred pounds, Ralph was playing on the line, both offense and defense.

The Bulldogs had been on the practice field for a quick walk-through practice just after noon before the varsity was to take the field that night for a home game. When the session was over, the players went to the locker room to shower and dress.

As he was taking off his jersey and shoulder pads, Ralph picked up a conversation on the other side of the bank of lockers.

"I'd sure like to take a run at Mary Dyke," one voice said. Ralph recognized it as Billy Steerman. "She's got a great body."

Ralph's protective ears went up, and he stopped what he was doing to listen in.

"Yeah, and she's probably pretty willing since her sister is too." Ralph could tell the other voice came from Bradley Taylor. Both boys in the conversation were sophomores, a year older than Ralph.

Still in his football pants and cleats, Ralph started to go around the bank of lockers to confront the two. As he walked, he heard more.

"What makes you think that?" Billy asked.

"Well, I heard she had quite a few guys in bed before they moved here," Bradley responded. "And the guy who supposedly beat her up was one of them."

By this time, Ralph was on their side of the room and stepped between them.

"Where are you hearing this crap about my sister?" he boomed. Other players in the locker room stopped what they were doing to see what the ruckus was.

"I just heard it around," Bradley said. "I don't remember who said it."

"It's bullshit, so you better stop spreading that around," Ralph hollered. "And stay away from Mary."

Billy, about Ralph's height but giving up about twenty pounds, stood chest to chest with him.

"I'll try to date whoever I want," he said. "And I'll do with them what I want."

Ralph reached out and shoved him backward. He lost his balance and fell into Billy. They both tumbled to the floor. The two boys scrambled to their feet and faced off with Ralph. The others in the locker room stood motionless, watching the scene. Others who were in different areas of the room gathered in the small space between lockers.

With all the attention on them, Billy and Bradley felt the stress most young boys feel at their age to not be pushed around by anyone. Bradley was two inches shorter than Ralph and thirty pounds lighter. But the testosterone flowing through him made him believe he was not overmatched. It was a mistake.

"Mary's probably just as willing as your other sister. She'll be easy—" Bradley could not even finish the sentence before Ralph's right fist crashed into his jaw, sending him sprawling on the floor again.

Ralph followed the punch by reaching down to pull Bradley up by the T-shirt with his left hand and leveling another punch at Bradley's head. But it was interrupted by Billy's arm that hooked Ralph's to stop it just inches away. Ralph grabbed him with both hands and lifted him off the floor then tossed him across the space between lockers.

Billy's head struck the hard metal of one of the locker handles, and he went down hard. Ralph had turned back to Bradley, ready to give him a few more shots to the head, so he didn't see that Billy went limp and that the blood started to flow from a cut on the back of his head.

Bradley used Ralph's attention to Billy to regain his feet, and when Ralph turned around, he saw Bradley's fist headed for his nose. He turned in time to take just a glancing blow, but it enraged him further, and he threw an uppercut into Bradley's belly. There was a loud groan and *whoosh* as the air went out of his lungs, and he collapsed, gasping for air.

It was then and only then that other players stepped in and held Ralph back. It took six of them, mostly other linemen, to keep him from going after the two boys who had spoken so disrespectfully about his sisters. It was then that two coaches, line coach Ed Mercer and varsity head coach Blane Swearingin, came running into the area.

"What the hell is going on here?" Swearingin bellowed.

"They were insulting my sisters, calling them whores!" Ralph yelled.

Coach Mercer was tending to Billy, still lying on the floor and the pool of blood getting larger. As Coach Mercer placed a towel over the wound and applied pressure, Coach Swearingin took charge of the locker room.

"The rest of you guys get your showers done and get dressed," he said. "Dyke, you come with me."

"I wasn't going to let them keep talking about my sisters like that," Ralph said, close to tears now.

"We'll find out what happened here, but right now, you need to come with me to the principal's office," the coach said and took him by the arm, leading him out of the room.

Ralph paused in his confession to his father. Bob tried hard to hide his own rage toward the two players who had said things about his daughters. If he were to admit the truth, he was proud of his son for standing up to them and defending their honor. If he had been in Ralph's shoes, Bob was certain he would have reacted in much the same way.

But he wanted his children to present themselves in a different way—to be patient and kind to people and to avoid violence. He also knew, though, it was easier said than done when faced with situations like his son experienced in that locker room. It was a lesson he learned early in life when he got in trouble for outbursts of violent retaliation to bullying he experienced and witnessed when he was in high school, and he was learning it again through his son.

There had been a few incidents at the mill in which he overheard some workers commenting on his family's situation. Some had questioned whether there was something to the whisperings around town prior to the attack on Sherry about her being sexually open to boys because of her past in Wyoming.

Bob had been tempted to smack the rumor mongers in the mouth. But he resisted, through a huge effort on his part. He related that to his son.

"I know, Dad. But it's hard to stand there and listen to things like that being said about Sherry and Mary," Ralph said.

Bob put a hand on his son's shoulder.

"I know it is, trust me," he said. "But it is doubly important for us now to exercise restraint, especially with this hearing coming up on Monday."

Ralph hung his head.

"Well, about that hearing, I might have made that worse too," he said.

"How do you mean?" Bob asked, concerned.

"When I was talking to the principal, he asked me about Sherry's case, and I mentioned the hearing," Ralph said. "He already knew about it, but he asked me if I knew Ted and how I felt about him."

Ralph paused, but his father squeezed his shoulder, indicating for him to go on.

"I was mad, Dad. I was still mad about what happened in the locker room," he said.

"So what did you say?" Bob asked.

"I told him I wanted to take Ted out into the woods and beat him to death," Ralph said.

Bob flashed back to his own thoughts about Ted and marveled at how similar they were to his son's.

"Don't worry about that," Bob said. "There are a lot of people who feel like that."

Ralph breathed in deeply, held it for a moment, then let it out.

"But I do worry, Dad," he said. "What if things I've said or done get used in court to get that asshole—" Ralph stopped short at his use of the swear word. He had never sworn in front of his parents before. "Sorry, Dad," he said.

Bob nodded and squeezed his son's shoulder again. This time, it was a reassuring squeeze.

"It's all right. I understand," was all he could say.

"But I don't want to be the cause, even in a small way, for that guy to get off scot-free," Ralph said.

"I don't think that will happen," Bob said, not really as convinced as he hoped he sounded. "They have to base their decision on the facts of what happened. And that is that Ted Brennen raped and beat your sister."

Ralph nodded and fell silent. Bob could tell that the conversation was at an end, and even though he didn't say it, Ralph now wanted to be alone. He gave his son a short man-to-man hug and left the room.

Karen's 1957 Chevy Bel Air glided across the Bridge of the Gods Saturday and eventually onto I-80 headed west. She and Sherry were headed to Portland for a day together.

Karen had driven to Carson from the University of Puget Sound the night before. She, like Barry, arranged to miss her Monday classes so she could be with her friend during the court hearing scheduled for that day.

They planned to spend some time shopping at Lloyd Center. Situated in the center of the city, the open-air shopping mall was the biggest in the Pacific Northwest when it was built in 1960 and still was a giant draw for shoppers in the Portland-Vancouver metro areas and the outlying areas as far away as Eastern Oregon and Washington.

Neither young woman was looking to buy anything specific, but the shopping trip was a good excuse to get out of Carson and spend some time together. Barry offered to go with them, but Karen wanted some time with Sherry to herself, and he agreed. But they all agreed that he would meet them at the mall in the late afternoon, and they would all go see a movie together.

After spending time in several stores, with no purchases, the girls decided to have a little lunch. Karen took advantage of the opportunity to address some concerns she had about her friend.

"How are you doing with all this stuff coming up with Ted's court hearing?" she asked.

Sherry had just taken a bite of her turkey sandwich and took advantage of the mouthful to give some thought to the question as she chewed.

In the weeks since she started physical therapy, she had worked very hard. She wanted to get back to what she had been before the attack. She was very driven to do so. Not only was she eager to be able to complete her enrollment application to Eastern Oregon State College so she could be with Barry, she wanted to do it to show Ted and those few who supported him that she was not going to buckle under and give up.

But there was a part of her that was afraid of the legal outcome. What if the judge decided not to go ahead with a trial and set him free? What if it did go to trial and he was found not guilty and got his freedom that way? Would he then continue his harassment of her? Would she be in danger of another attack?

All those possibilities swirled around in her head on a daily basis. While she wasn't going to let her doubts blunt her desire to improve her physical condition, she was concerned about her safety.

"I am nervous," she finally said after swallowing.

"I'm sure you are," Karen responded. "But I don't think you have much to worry about."

It wasn't exactly what Karen was thinking, but she wanted to reassure her friend. Karen had also been nurturing the same concerns as Sherry. And she could not help remembering their conversation in which Sherry described what she would like to see happen to her tormentor.

"But what if he does get away with this?" Sherry asked. "How safe will I be?"

"I think he's going to spend a lot of time in jail," Karen said then paused to push a few french fries into her mouth and quickly chewed and swallowed them. "But even if he does get out of jail, right away or later, he'd have to know that anything he did to threaten you would just make it look like he was guilty all along."

"Getting to say 'I told you so' won't do me much good if he beats and rapes me again," Sherry said sarcastically after gulping down some soda.

"I didn't really mean that," Karen said, a little stung by Sherry's tone.

"Well, that's the way it would be," Sherry said. "If he's let out, he'll come after me. Maybe not right away, but any time would be too soon for me."

Karen could tell the conversation was uncomfortable for Sherry. But she was hurt by her friend's sarcastic retort. She had never been that way with her since they met. Their conversations had always been cordial. Their bond remained the same.

But Karen was now recognizing that in her time away at school, Sherry's attitude was different. There was more of an edge in her voice, even during their talks on the trip from Carson to Portland. She was sure Sherry's nervousness over the upcoming court hearing was a factor. But she couldn't help from letting her emotions get the better of her.

"There's no need to get so snippy with me," she said. "I'm just trying to be your friend and help as much as I can."

In addition to the physical therapy, Sherry had been undergoing some emotional counseling. One of the techniques used by the counselor, who traveled from Vancouver for her sessions with Sherry and others in the small communities of Stevenson and Carson, was to get Sherry to share her feelings toward her attacker. Those sessions had intensified as the court hearing drew closer.

Sherry's feelings of hatred for and desire for revenge against Ted came pouring out of her. She shared the same images she had done with Karen, but with the counselor, they were even more detailed and intense.

One of the counselor's goals were twofold. First, she wanted Sherry to face her emotions and find ways to deal with them in a less aggressive way. The other goal was to strengthen her self-confidence.

Without knowing how this had come about, because Sherry had not shared her counseling sessions with anyone, Karen was now seeing the results of those efforts.

"I'm sorry if you think I'm snippy, Karen," Sherry said. "I'm just trying to deal with all this the best that I can. Until you've been in my shoes, you have no clue what I'm going through."

Karen knew it was true. But that did not ease her hurt feelings. She saw a definite change in her friend. When they met and through the past year, Sherry had been someone who needed guidance in her new surroundings and Karen was the mentor. Karen was the dominant friend in the relationship. She could now see that changing.

Sherry had developed a hard shell, and she was becoming more independent. In some ways, Karen did not like the switch.

"Well, I'm never going to know exactly what you've been through unless someone rapes and beats me," Karen said with her own hard tone.

"I sure hope that never happens to you," Sherry said. This time, the sarcasm was missing. "I wouldn't wish that on anyone."

"Except maybe Ted?" Karen asked, referring to their earlier conversation.

Sherry sat silently for several minutes, not touching her food. She finally sucked a few mouthfuls of soda and swallowed them. She pushed her tray toward the middle of the small table, and it nudged Karen's tray.

"Yeah, I wish that son of a bitch could feel what I went through," she said angrily, "and then some. And if I could be the one to make sure he feels that, the better it would be."

The two did a little more shopping, but it was mostly in silence. Finally, they went to the theater and found Barry already there waiting. Pickings were slim, and they decided to see Big Bad Mama with Angie Dickinson, William Shatner, and Tom Skerrit.

Barry could see the tension between the girls from the moment they appeared in front of the theater. He decided not to pursue it at that time, hoping to be able to talk to Sherry later.

Chapter 13

With Ted's hearing just around the corner, the tension in the Dyke household was beginning to build. It began to ramp up with Sherry's trip to Portland with Karen on Saturday. It exploded in the Dyke family on Sunday.

The family tradition was to always gather for breakfast together on Sundays. With all the children in school and involved in activities, there were few times when they would all be together. But Sundays were a different story.

The Dykes were not institutionally religious. Bob and Katrina were what they called spiritual. Neither was certain about the existence of a supreme being, but both were suspicious of institutional religion. They wanted their children to find their own path regarding religion and encouraged them to explore all their options. So they had never gone to church regularly.

Bob enjoyed sports but was not as fanatic about it some, and Katrina only had a passing interest in sports. So watching pro football on television at this time of year, or any other sports during the rest of the year, was not a scheduled event. They watched if they were interested in the moment.

Mary had gone out for volleyball her freshman year and did so again her sophomore year. She also planned to play basketball. With

Ralph on the football team, Bob and Katrina focused their sports interests in their children.

Terry and Sherry had not participated in school sports.

That left Sundays free for all family members to be home. The three girls helped their mother prepare a traditional family breakfast, and Bob and his sons, before Terry left for the Navy and when he visited, were available to do whatever was necessary. This day, the family was preparing a standard bacon, eggs, and hash browns breakfast.

Mary was busy peeling the potatoes while Sherry was grating them into a bowl. They worked in silence for a few minutes until Mary spoke up.

"I kept getting boys asking me to go out with them the last several days, but that really hadn't happened that much before," she said quietly.

"Did you agree to go out with anyone?" Sherry asked. She was interested in Mary's responses because she wanted to do what she could to guide her through what appeared to be boys' increased desire to date her. She remembered when she was Mary's age and experienced a rise in attention from boys as she developed into a young woman.

"There were a couple that I would like to," she said.

"But you didn't say yes?" Sherry asked.

"I was going to say yes to one of them until all that ruckus with Ralph started going around," Mary answered.

"But why not go ahead?" Sherry asked.

"I wondered whether they were asking me out just because they thought I was easy," Mary said.

Sherry stopped grating in mid swipe.

"Why would you think that?" Sherry asked a little testily and loud enough that Kim and Katrina took notice.

"The boys that Ralph fought with said they thought so because I was your sister," Mary said clumsily, caught a bit off guard.

"Are you saying you think I'm easy?" Sherry asked angrily, dropping the grater and potato in her hands onto the counter. Kim and Katrina stopped what they were doing and looked toward the sisters.

"I didn't say that. They did," Mary said.

"But you must believe them. Otherwise, why would you hesitate about going out with someone you are interested in?" Sherry said.

Mary was beginning to feel some fright at her sister's accusations, but at the same time, she was getting a little angry with her.

Katrina moved away from the stove and got in between her daughters.

"That's enough," she said. "There is no need to be like this."

"But, Mom—" Sherry began, but her mother cut her off.

"No buts," Katrina said. "If you can't work together without sniping at each other, I'll fix that."

Katrina looked at Sherry. "You go set the table," she said. Then looking at Mary, she added, "You finish the potatoes."

With the hash browns just over half done, now Mary had to do both tasks. She was not happy.

"I'll help Mary," Kim said from the stove where she had been helping her mother.

"No, you'll keep doing what you are doing," Katrina said as she moved back beside her. Mary continued to peel potatoes, but now a little more aggressively. It did not go unnoticed by her mother. Katrina also noticed Sherry's anger, expressed in the rough way she handled the dishes and silverware as she set the table. But this was not the time to address it, she thought.

During breakfast preparation, Bob and Ralph were in the backyard, making a show of trimming the weeds in the area behind the house. In reality, Bob was taking the opportunity to talk to his son about Friday's events.

Little had been said to the younger Dyke in the previous two days. Bob knew his son well and that trying to confront the issue immediately after the fact would only enflame Ralph's emotions, which Bob knew were quite high. How could he know otherwise? He shared his son's infuriation toward the two boys who had spoken so callously about his eldest daughters.

That was, in fact, another reason he decided to wait to talk with Ralph. The boy was his father's son, after all. They shared many qualities, including their deep feelings and emotions.

"You know fighting those boys was not the best response to what they said about Mary and Sherry, right?" he asked as he ran the Weedwacker along the base of the house, and Ralph picked up the fallen remnants.

"Dad, I can't stand people talking that way about my sisters," he said with a hint of defensiveness in his voice. "None of them."

"That wasn't what I asked," Bob said evenly.

It was a few seconds before Ralph responded.

"I know that I should not have hit them the way that I did."

Bob could tell that Ralph understood that his reaction was inappropriate, but he could tell by the tone of his voice there was no remorse in the response.

"What would you have done in that situation, Dad?" Ralph asked.

Bob had to choke back the response he would have given if he spoke the truth. He thought back to the instance with the first interview with Deputies Whisnofski and Pyle. His anger had gotten the better of him, and he had said things that could come back to haunt him later if anything happened to Ted. He regretted losing his temper, but at the same time, he knew his thoughts at that moment could very well be his reaction.

For that reason, and other actions in his far past, he knew if he had been in Ralph's shoes, his reaction would have been much the same. But he knew as a father that he could not let his son know that. But at the same time, he could not lie to him.

"I would hope that I would take a measured approach, maybe say something about what they said was false, and then go to the principal to report it," Bob took what he thought was a middle ground.

Ralph wasn't buying it.

"You said you hoped you would do that," he said. "But it sounds to me like you're not sure."

Bob shut off the Weedwacker and leaned against the house a few seconds before responding.

"I don't think any of us are 100 percent sure how we would handle stressful or confrontational situations," he finally said. Ralph started to say something, but Bob cut him off with a raised hand, palm facing forward. "That does not mean we should let our emotions guide our actions," he said. "We have to understand that violence is not the best way to solve problems."

"I understand that, Dad," Ralph said. "You and Mom have taught us all that."

Bob felt a twang of pride. It is always heartwarming for a parent to hear one of their children affirm that what they were trying to teach their children is actually getting through.

"But it is really hard when I hear something like that about anyone in the family," Ralph said.

"Life is not easy, son, and we all have to face situations that test us," Bob said.

"And I failed this test," Ralph said sadly.

Bob reached out and put his hand on his son's shoulder.

"That's true, but what really matters now is how you move on from it," Bob said. He then pulled Ralph into his arms and gave him a tight hug.

"I'm always proud of you, Ralph, and I know you will do the right thing," he said.

Katrina had appeared at the back door to call Bob and Ralph into breakfast just as the two embraced. She said nothing for a few moments to let the two continue the bond. Bob was facing the back of the house and caught sight of his wife in the doorway. Their gazes locked on each other, and a tear rolled down on each of their cheeks.

Not long after an uncharacteristically silent breakfast, Ralph was in his room getting ready to go for a run. Despite being suspended from school, he still wanted to stay in shape for when he was able to return to the football team.

As he was tying his sneakers, Kim walked by then doubled back and timidly stepped into her brother's room. While she had heard about the trouble he had gotten into at school, no one had shared the details with her. Curiosity was consuming her.

Kim had not been let in on all the reasons why they had to make the sudden move from Wyoming. Her parents simply told her Bob had a job opportunity in another state. But even at nine years old, she heard things around town before they left. She knew their move had something to do with her oldest sister. Now just as they had settled into their new home and she had made new friends, Sherry had been beaten up, and Kim was afraid they would be moving again.

Because her parents had not shared with her the full truth about what happened in Wyoming nor the full extent of what happened to Sherry this time, she knew nothing about the rapes.

Ralph looked up to see his younger sister standing just inside his room's doorway with a questioning look on her face.

"Hi, Kim, what's up?" he asked, now finished with his sneakers.

She took a step forward and lowered her gaze to the floor.

"Are we going to be moving again?" she asked.

The question caught Ralph off guard, and he hesitated.

"Why would we be moving?" he asked.

"Well, you got in trouble at school," she said.

"Why would that mean we would move again?" he asked, still trying to figure out what had prompted her to think the family would abandon their new home.

"Well, Sherry got in some kind of trouble in Wyoming, and we moved here," she answered.

For an instant, Ralph got a little angry. Why was he being blamed for a new turmoil in the family? He hadn't done anything near as bad as had been done to Sherry; therefore, there would be no reason for the family to walk away from this new home and life they were building.

He was about to express all those thoughts when it suddenly struck him. This wasn't about him; it was about Kim. And in some ways, it was also about Sherry.

He knew that Kim was left in the dark concerning the details of what drove the family out of Wyoming. He could not imagine how confused she was. And for the first time, Ralph suddenly understood how Sherry must have felt, and was still feeling, about the difficulties the family was going through. He now understood the guilt she must be dealing with, because for that instant of anger, he felt the burden of guilt on his shoulders like a fully loaded truck.

"We're not going to move again," Ralph said, motioning for Kim to come sit beside him on the bed. She did so, but the look of bewilderment never left her face.

"What I did and what happened to Sherry are very different things," Ralph continued. "I got in a fight, and what happened to Sherry, both in Wyoming and here, are very different things."

"Because she is the one who got beat up instead of being the one that was beating up on someone else?" Kim asked.

"Something like that, but it's a bit more complicated," her brother answered.

"What do you mean?" Kim asked.

Ralph paused for a moment. He wasn't real comfortable talking about the details of what happened to Sherry with Kim. For one thing, he wasn't sure he would express it in a way that an eleven-year-old would understand. For another, he believed it was better for his parents to discuss that part of the issue with her.

"What I did Friday was wrong," he began. "I got angry and acted on that anger instead of controlling myself and handling it another way."

"What made you so angry?" Kim asked. "Does it have something to do with this court thing tomorrow?"

Again, Ralph took a moment to collect his thoughts before answering.

"Yes, in a way," he finally answered. "Those boys I hit were saying bad things about Sherry and Mary."

"What kind of bad things?" she asked.

Now a bit of frustration was setting in for Ralph. It seemed as much as he tried, he was either going to have to address the sexual aspect of the issue with his younger sister or find a way to deflect the conversation to his parents. He knew that Kim had still not passed into adolescence. With his older sisters, it had been plainly obvious when they got their first periods and the so-called facts of life were explained to them by their mother. That had not yet happened with Kim.

"How much do you know about sex?" he asked, deciding to just dine in and try to do his best.

"I know that's how babies are made," she said and raised her head to look her brother in the eyes. "And I know that boys have something they put in the girl to do it."

Ralph smiled inwardly at the simplicity of her knowledge. But it also made him a little nervous not knowing just how much information to give her. He still believed it was not his place to be giving that birds and bees talk.

"Well, someone tried to do that to Sherry in Wyoming and she didn't want him to," Ralph said. "And then someone tried to do the same here. Only this time, he did more than try to have sex with her."

"He beat her up because she wouldn't, right?" Kim asked.

"Something like that," Ralph said.

"Why would two guys try to do that if she didn't want to?" Kim asked.

Ralph had no real answer for that question because it was something he wondered himself.

"I don't know. Some guys are just like that," he said. "And it wasn't two guys. It was the same one. A guy named Ted that Sherry dated for a little while in Wyoming."

It was at that moment that Sherry happened to walk by and hear Ralph's last statement to Kim. Neither Ralph nor Kim saw her standing in the doorway until she shouted at her brother.

"What the hell are you telling her?"

Startled, Ralph and Kim looked up to see their sister in full rage.

"You have no right talking to her or anyone else about me!" Sherry screamed.

"She came in here asking me questions. I wasn't going to lie to her," Ralph said as he stood up, determined to stand his ground.

"You should have sent her to me or to Mom and Dad!" Sherry said, still screaming.

Kim, still sitting on Ralph's bed, began to sob. He sat back down and put his arm around her and tried to soothe her.

"Maybe, but at the time, I didn't want her to be any more confused," Ralph said. "Besides, she was asking about me and what happened Friday."

"That's bullshit. I heard you telling her about Ted and what he did to me!" Sherry yelled.

"It was all connected," Ralph said.

Before he or Sherry could say another word, they heard Bob's voice as he bounded up the stairs with Katrina and Mary right behind him.

"What the hell is going on up here?"

Ralph got up and headed toward the door. Sherry stepped back into the hallway and faced her parents. Kim stayed seated on the bed, now crying harder.

"This jerk is telling Kim all about what's happened to me!" Sherry said, toning her voice down a few decibels, but still shouting. Ralph had since stepped into the hallway.

"Kim came in and asked me if we were going to move because of what happened Friday," he said. "She was afraid that would happen because we moved from Wyoming after trouble there." He was careful not to mention Sherry in his opening defending statement.

"That's ridiculous. How could anyone think that?" Sherry said, lowering her voice a bit more.

"That's enough, Sherry," her father said. She was a little taken aback. "Ralph, you and Kim come downstairs. Sherry and Mary, you stay up here until we call you."

The Dyke family was arranged around the dining table. Sherry and Mary were on opposite corners, Ralph and Kim sat on the same side of the table as Mary, and Bob and Katrina were at each end. Bob surveyed the scene and motioned for Kim to come sit at the corner nearest him. She looked at her brother, who nodded ever so slightly, and she complied.

They sat in silence for a few moments. Sherry stared at the tabletop in front of her, not wanting to look at Mary or Ralph. Mary looked at her father, also not wanting to meet Sherry's eyes. Kim was scared, despite what her parents had said in a conversation with her and Ralph just before this gathering.

Ralph, who now sat with a look of great concern on his face, had given his parents that facts of his conversation with Kim in his room. During that brief meeting with just the four of them, Kim only acknowledged his explanation with nods. Despite her parents' assurances, she remained worried that they would be uprooting themselves and moving to a new community.

When that meeting was over, Bob looked at Katrina, and she knew exactly what he planned as their next move. Now they were gathered around the family dining table to carry it out.

Bob broke the silence that was as thick and solid as the concrete that made up the Bonneville Dam just a couple of miles down the Columbia River.

"We've got some problems in the family that need to be resolved," he said. "And we're not leaving this table until they are."

He glanced at each of his children in turn. "Well, who wants to start?" he asked.

They all sat still, maintaining the same posture and stone-cold silence. Just before Bob was about to take the matter into his own hands, Kim spoke up.

"I don't want for us to move away again," she said hesitantly.

Bob looked at her with tenderness.

"Why would you think we're going to be moving?" he asked.

Kim hesitated and stole a glance at Sherry, who turned her head to glare at her.

"Because there was trouble in Wyoming and we moved, and Friday, there was more trouble," she said, careful not to mention any names in hopes of avoiding Sherry's wrath. She was certain Ralph would hold no malice toward her for bringing up his incident in detail.

Sherry started to say something, but her father silenced her with an upward extended index finger.

"I can assure you, we will not be moving anytime soon for any reason," he said, panning the table then looking at Kim. "We're here to stay. Do you believe me?"

Kim nodded slowly. She believed her father was convinced that what he was saying was true. And that was good enough for her.

"Good," Bob said. "One problem resolved." He turned to Mary to his left. Her eyes had stayed on him the entire time he was dealing with Kim's issue.

"Sherry accused me of calling her easy, and that's not at all what I said," she told her father.

"That is exactly—" Sherry started, but without taking his eyes off his second daughter, Bob held out the upturned index finger again, and she went silent.

"What did you say?" he asked.

"We were talking about boys asking me out, and I said there were some who did and a couple I would like to go out with, but I didn't because the boys Ralph fought with said they wanted to have sex with me," she blurted out and then fell silent.

"And?" Bob prodded her.

"Sherry asked why I didn't go out with them, and I said it was because of what those boys said, that they were interested in me just because I was Sherry's sister," she stammered.

"You see—" Sherry started again, but the upturned index finger put an end to it again.

"Can you see why she might be offended by that?" Bob asked Mary.

She thought about it for a few moments before responding.

"I suppose I can see why she would think that's what they were calling her, but I did not say or even think that at all," Mary said firmly.

Bob's only response was to point toward Sherry. Mary knew exactly what he was getting at. She turned to face her older sister.

"I do not think you are easy," she said with as much sympathy in her tone as she could muster. "I know that nothing that has happened to you was done because you gave permission for it. You've gone through some horrible things, and I wish with all my heart that it had never happened."

Sherry's hardened look softened ever so slightly.

"If I could make it all go away, I would," Mary continued. "I would never do anything that I thought would be hurtful to you."

Both girls began to tear up.

"Two problems resolved," Bob said then looked to Ralph before Sherry could respond.

"I don't know what Sherry thought I was doing by talking to Kim, but I was only trying to answer her questions as best I could," he said.

"It really wasn't your—" Sherry started to say before her father's index finger was in the air again. Ralph looked his sister in the eyes.

"There were things I tried to explain to Kim that were more appropriate for Mom and Dad to talk to her about," he began. Then he continued, "But she was very scared and very worried and very confused, and I didn't want to leave her hanging."

Sherry wiped a tear from one eye and then another but held her voice after glancing at her father with his poised index finger.

"There's nothing I wouldn't do to make things better for you," Ralph said. "But Friday wasn't the smartest thing to do. I'm sorry if that causes any problems for you."

"Three problems solved," Bob said before anyone could speak again. He then looked at Sherry. Assuming it was her turn to speak, she opened her mouth, but this time, her father held his hand out with the palm facing her.

"Sherry, you have been through hell and back in the last couple of years, and we all wish we could make it all go away," Bob said. "But unfortunately, we can't do that, and we have to play on with the cards we were dealt."

He paused to choke back a lump in his throat from thinking about the pain she must have endured through both incidents with Ted.

"There isn't anyone, I mean anyone, who cares about you more than the people in this room, at this table," Bob continued. "We will get through this. But to do it, we have to be there for each other. You need to be there for us just like we'll be there for you. Because while you took the brunt of all this, we are all hurting right along with you."

He then extended his hand to her with the palm facing up, indicating it was her turn to talk. Sherry felt the stare of five sets of eyes boring down on her, waiting anxiously for her response. The anger was still within her, but it was no longer directed toward her family members.

"This has been very hard on me," she finally said then paused to see the anxious faces looking at her. "But I know it has been hard on all of you too. Probably harder in some ways because you can't make it better for me."

The collective sighs of relief around the table were inaudible, but it showed in their faces.

"I'm sorry to all of you for being such a...," she started to say then stopped herself.

"Go ahead," her mother spoke for the first time.

"I'm sorry for being such a cranky ass bitch," Sherry said.

Everyone at the table, including Bob and Katrina, broke out in hearty laughter. Sherry remained stoic for a second or two then joined in.

"Four problems resolved," Bob said as the laughter died down.

"From now on, if we have a problem with each other, we talk it out," he continued. "If you just can't talk to each other, come to us and we will help."

He looked around the table. "Agreed?" They all nodded.

"Five problems resolved," Bob said.

Chapter 14

Ted's pretrial hearing was scheduled to begin at nine o'clock in the morning, and Judge Belfor's gavel banged down on the Portland Buckaroos hockey puck exactly at that time.

The Dyke family had been there since before eight o'clock. Shaw spent some time briefing them about what to expect in the proceedings. He explained that the hearing was to determine whether the case should proceed to trial. That decision would be made by the judge.

While Shaw did explain to the Dykes that it was possible the defense attorney could make an offer for a deal in which Ted would face less severe charges if he changed his plea to guilty, he also let them know that if a deal was proposed and accepted, Ted's punishment would be less than it would be otherwise.

"Then we don't want any deals," Bob said sternly.

Shaw had been through enough of these proceedings that he was prepared for this reaction.

"We could take that stance, Bob, but if we aren't open to any kind of deal and things don't work out our way at trial, he could go unpunished," Shaw said.

"So are you saying you don't have enough confidence in this case to fight hard enough to get that jackass put in jail where he belongs?" Bob asked testily.

Shaw sighed. This, too, was a situation he had faced many times before.

"If you're not up to the job, there should be another prosecutor that can get it done," Bob continued.

"Well, Bob, we can go that route if you really want to, but that means whoever takes my place will be coming in cold with very little time to prepare," Shaw said. "Mr. Brennen has been in jail a longer time than it usually takes to get to this point because we delayed as much as possible until Sherry was further along in her recovery."

"So now you're blaming her," Bob said as his anger rose. Sherry reached out and touched her father's arm, and he calmed slightly.

The remark stung deeply for Shaw. This case was one that he took a special interest in because of the brutality of the crimes. He despised bullies, and it was clear that Ted Brennen was a particularly cruel one. This was a case he wanted to win badly and get the harshest punishment possible for the suspect in the end.

So to be accused of not having the confidence or skills to pull it off was one thing, but to then be accused of trying to blame the victim got his anger stirred up.

But being the experienced prosecutor that he was, he knew he had to stay calm and not let his emotions get the best of him at all times and especially with the victim and her family.

"No, Bob, I'm not blaming her at all," Shaw said gently. "All I'm saying is that because he's been in there longer than normal, it may work against us with the judge."

The prosecutor turned to Sherry.

"You are the main victim in this case," he said. "What are your wishes?"

The room went silent, and the only sound for a few moments was the ticking of the wall clock over the door. All eyes in the room focused on Sherry. Finally, she spoke up.

"I want him to get the punishment he deserves for what he did to me," she said. "If that means going to trial, then that's what we should do."

"What is it you think he deserves as punishment?" Shaw asked.

Sherry was again silent for a moment.

"What I want I know the judge won't allow," she said. "So I want the most the law will allow."

Shaw smiled. It was certainly the direction he wanted to go. He was confident in the case he had built with the evidence he had. But at the same time, he could not become overconfident. As he told the family earlier, the outcome was not a foregone conclusion by any means.

But now that he knew where Sherry wanted to go with the case, that was not something he wanted to project to this family. He wanted them going into that courtroom filled with the idea that they were going to see the outcome they were hoping for—a trial and conviction.

Now he turned to the task of briefing each of the family members he intended to call as witnesses.

The purpose of a preliminary hearing is to determine if there is enough evidence to necessitate a trial. In such a hearing, the burden of proof is on the prosecution. The state will present its case using the evidence and witnesses it has gathered. The defense attorney is allowed to cross-examine the witnesses, but since it is incumbent on the prosecutor to prove the need for a trial, they typically ask few, if any, questions of witnesses.

A preliminary hearing is also a balancing act for the state because the prosecutor does not want to give away too much of his case, but he must present enough to convince the judge to order a trial. If too much is revealed, the defense will be able to see the prosecutor's strategy and be able to counter it.

This was all on Bill Shaw's mind as the judge's gavel opened the session. Legal proceedings are very much like chess games where strategy and sacrifice are major factors.

"Is the state ready to proceed?" Belfor asked of Shaw.

"We are, Your Honor," he answered.

He stood and walked to the front of the prosecution table and began. He described the Dyke family, mentioning each member's name, but not looking back toward them. He talked briefly about the family's time in Wyoming, explaining that Bob was a mill worker and that Katrina was a homemaker. He told of the five children, making it a point to tell how the oldest son, Terry, had enlisted in the Navy.

Next, he moved into the part of the family's story when they left Wyoming and came to Washington.

"Sherry Dyke had become smitten with a man older than her, a man already out of high school and with a little more real-world experience than herself," Shaw said. "No doubt that was appealing to her."

He glanced back at Sherry, sitting at the end of the first row behind the prosecutor's table. She gave him a sorrowful, regretful nod. It was a piece of theater he had worked out with her for the judge's benefit.

"Mr. Brennen, on the other hand, was known for pursuing younger girls as a matter of control," Shaw said, turning back to the bench.

"I object, conjecture," Keith Ryan said from the defense table. Ted, sitting to his left, sat staring straight ahead, but with a look of disgust as a mask.

"We have depositions that show not only a pattern of pursuing younger girls but of abuse," Shaw said before Belfor could respond.

"And we have not had the opportunity to depose these so-called witnesses," Ryan said.

It was a weak argument, and Ryan knew it. During preliminary hearings, the rules are a little different than during a trial. Some evidence that could not be heard in a trial would be allowed during a preliminary hearing. But it was his way to let Shaw know he would not get away with using the depositions if there was a trial. He would have to allow the defense to cross-examine the deposed witnesses if it came to that.

"Go ahead, Mr. Shaw," Belfor said, not even acknowledging Ryan's last plea.

"Sherry had refused a few attempts by Mr. Brennen to engage in sex," Shaw said, knowing things were going to be emotional for the Dyke family from here on. "But one night, he was not going to take no for an answer."

He gave a quick glance to the defense table, trying to match Ted's look of disgust with his own.

"He raped her," he said, still looking at the defense table to see Ryan begin to stand and object. "Excuse me, he allegedly raped her in his Ford Mustang."

As a result of the act, Shaw went on, "Sherry became pregnant. But she did not want to keep the baby, a product of an act she neither wanted nor willingly participated in. She and her parents decided on an abortion. That led to harassment in the small town, and they decided they could no longer live there and came west." Shaw concluded that part of the saga.

"The family settled in Carson and became well accepted into the community," Shaw said. "And then Mr. Brennen showed up."

Shaw had gone back to his chair behind the prosecution table. He fingered several items in front of him—the blood samples, grass clipping, the handkerchief, a pair of red men's bikini underwear. He paused over these items for a few moments, looking down at them.

"Shortly after Mr. Brennen's arrival, Sherry was again raped and this time brutally beaten," he said, looking up at the judge.

He explained that three people had abducted Sherry while she walked home from the store. They had blindfolded her before she could get a look at any of them and took her to a spot just outside Carson.

"Two of the men held her while an unknown subject," he said, looking straight at Ted, "raped her. When she fought back, this subject"—he continued to stare at Ted, who was still staring straight ahead—"and the others beat her so badly that both her legs were broken, an arm was broken, and created severe internal damage."

Shaw could hear sobs coming from each member of the Dyke family. But he pressed on.

"Despite being blindfolded, Sherry was able to ascertain that blindfold was a red pattern handkerchief," he said, holding up the garment recovered near the clearing by Whisnofski and Pyle's latest search there. "She saw the subject was wearing men's red bikini underwear." He held up, holding it at arm's length, the underwear in question. "And we have blood samples taken from the scene that match the blood of Sherry Dyke," he said, holding up the evidence envelopes and the test results.

He explained the handkerchief was found near the attack scene and that similar handkerchiefs were found in Ted's small apartment. He also told the judge the underwear was recovered from the same apartment.

"Those items are commonly sold in stores," Ryan said in objection. "If we did a search of all the homes in Carson and Stevenson, we'd find them in at least half the homes."

Shaw knew that argument would be made, and he had little to counter it. But he proceeded with what he had.

"That is true," he began. "But Sherry recognized the voice of her main attacker. She knew it well, having dated him before and… allegedly…been raped by him before."

Again, he looked at Ted, still staring straight ahead as if in a trance.

"It was the voice of Ted Brennen," he said.

Shaw sat down in the seat behind his table and glanced at his notes. He didn't need to look at them, but it gave him a chance to shift gears in his mind as he was preparing to call some witnesses. He also hoped the pause would allow for Ryan to make some arguments, but he remained silent.

"Mr. Shaw, do you have any witnesses to call?" Judge Belfor asked.

"Yes, Your Honor. I call Jim Brewster to the stand," Shaw answered.

After Jim had taken his seat in the witness box, Shaw had him describe finding Sherry on the side of the highway early on the morning of the attack upon her. Shaw then called Helen Brewster to the stand and had her describe the incident, which was a dead-on match to her husband's account.

Bob Dyke was the next one on the witness stand.

"It is your contention that Ted Brennen raped Sherry in Wyoming, is that correct?" he asked.

"That is correct," Bob said.

"Why are you so certain?" Shaw asked.

"Because my daughter said it happened, and I believe her," Bob answered.

"Why did you believe her?" Shaw asked. "In most cases, when teenagers get into trouble, they find any story to support a version that would absolve them of any wrongdoing."

Bob looked as though he had been kicked in the groin. Shaw had briefed him about this line of questioning, but he was so certain his children would not take that path; the remark still riled him.

"We have taught our children that telling the truth is one of the most important things in life," Bob said. He was beginning to feel frustration building within him.

"That is commendable," Shaw said. "But how do you know she was telling the truth on this occasion?"

"None of our children have ever given us any reason to doubt their truthfulness," Bob said. "My daughter said she was raped in Wyoming and in Washington, and I believe her without question."

Shaw turned to Judge Belfor and was about to say he had no more questions when he heard Bob's voice from the witness box.

"And that bastard did it both times," he said, pointing angrily to Ted.

With all eyes but Bob's and Ted's on the witness stand, Ted, still looking straight ahead, put his right hand to his face with only the middle finger extended.

"You smug son of a bitch," Bob said, rising from his chair and starting to go around the partition in front of it. But he was grabbed by a bailiff and held fast.

Judge Belfor banged his gavel.

"That will be enough!" he yelled. When there was silence in the room, he went on, "Mr. Dyke, if you cannot control yourself, I will have you removed from this courtroom, do you understand?"

Bob opened his mouth to tell the judge what Ted had done, but Shaw silenced him with a harsh look.

"Yes, I understand," he said with anger dripping from the words.

Silence returned to the courtroom as the bailiff escorted Bob to his seat. Katrina took his hand and squeezed it supportively. They looked into each other's eyes, both beginning to tear up. All the children rallied around him, hugging him and patting him on the back.

"Little jerk flipped me off," he whispered just loud enough so they all could hear but the judge could not. Shaw did catch the comment and filed it away for future use.

"We'll take a fifteen-minute break to allow everyone to calm down a bit," the judge said, rapped his gavel, and left the courtroom.

Shaw was pretty peeved as he paced back and forth in front of the Dyke family seated in the anteroom. Shaw talked as he paced.

"When I briefed you earlier, did I not say to stay calm when you are on the stand?" he asked rhetorically. He glanced at them to see they were either nodding or hanging their heads—all but Bob. Shaw could tell he had something to say. He stopped pacing and looked him in the eye expectantly.

"He flipped me off," Bob said. "He put his head in his hand, but he had his middle finger up."

"Yes, I heard you say that in the courtroom," Shaw said. "And that could be something we can use."

Bob seemed vindicated, but Shaw snapped that mood.

"You lost it before that may or may not have happened," Shaw said. "It's likely no one else saw it because they were focused on you."

That was something Bob had not considered.

"But no matter what happens, you—none of you—can lose your cool," Shaw said. "If we can use his antics against him, they can use your outbursts against us."

"So what now?" Ralph asked. "Can we fix this?"

Shaw pulled a chair away from the conference table the family was sitting around and sat down.

"When we go back out there, I'll go through the attempt to question Mr. Brennen and how he ran away," Shaw explained. "After that, I'll call Mary up to tell about how she saw him stalking your house."

He stopped and looked at Sherry.

"Then I'm going to have you describe what happened to you," he said. "Are you up for that?"

His question was not so much out of concern for Sherry's well-being. He knew that her testimony was key, and she had to give it for there to be any chance of getting the case to a trial. Instead, he wanted to see her reaction.

"I'm ready. I can handle it. I won't break," Sherry said. Sitting next to her father, she reached out and took his hand in hers, gave it a squeeze, and smiled at him, as if to say, "Don't worry, Dad. I don't mean you were wrong in losing it." He smiled back at her but still felt guilty. He hoped it didn't show.

Shaw hoped she was right but was not totally convinced. He had seen and heard from the deputies about the intense emotions of this family, including Sherry. But he was impressed with how she had handled the situation from the attack onward. So he was ready to proceed with confidence that she could keep her emotions in check on the witness stand.

She had to. It could make all the difference.

Chapter 15

Skamania County Sheriff's Deputy Jeremy Stone was on the witness stand describing his attempt to question Ted following the attack on Sherry.

"I went to his apartment in Home Valley and knocked on his door, identifying myself as a deputy," he said. "It took a few minutes, but he finally came to the door. He opened the door but left the screen door shut."

He paused for a moment then continued.

"I told him I wanted to ask him a few questions about an incident in Carson," the deputy said. "At first, he seemed willing to cooperate. But when I mentioned Sherry Dyke's name, he slammed the door, and I heard the dead bolt engage. I tried to open the screen door, but it was also locked."

He glanced over at the defense table to see Ted staring straight ahead, no expression on his face.

"I instructed my partner, Bruce Madison, to check the back to see if there was a rear entry," Stone went on. "His apartment was a triplex, and his was in the middle, so it took Bruce a while to get around. I heard him yell stop, and then I heard a car start up and peel out."

"Was it Mr. Brennen?" Shaw asked.

"Yes. He drove around the east side of the triplex and headed for the river highway," Madison said. "Bruce came back around, and he got in our cruiser. But by that time, the suspect was headed west toward Stevenson and was ahead of us by about a half mile."

"Did someone else join the chase?" Shaw asked.

"Yes, a Grand Prix got between the suspect's Mustang and us at the junction where the diner is," Madison said. "We later found out it was Barry Walker, the victim's boyfriend."

Stone then described how they were cut off by the truck on the north end of the Bridge of the Gods. By the time they were clear of it, Ted's car had gone off the road and Barry had apprehended him.

Bruce Madison followed his partner on the stand and gave the same description of events.

Mary was quite nervous as she took her place in the witness stand. She had always feared Ted. Being quite older, she knew of him by reputation. People in her Wyoming hometown talked about his treatment of women as objects, and those who were attracted to him, he treated like property.

When Sherry began dating him, she asked her sister what it was that attracted her to him. She had heard the same stories Mary had. Sherry could not give a logical reason; it was something she couldn't explain. But she had confided in her sister that while she was attracted to him, she was also afraid to break it off.

With everything that had transpired since then, she understood why people were afraid of Ted. So on the witness stand, she tried to avoid looking in his direction. But Shaw wasn't going to make that easy.

"You said there was a man stalking your house," he asked gently. She replied that was true. "Can you identify this man?"

Without looking in his direction, Mary pointed toward Ted.

"I need you to tell us, for the record, Miss Dyke," Judge Belfor said softly from the bench.

"It was Ted Brennen, the man sitting at the defense table," she said in a barely audible whisper.

"I didn't quite catch that," Ryan stood and said.

The sound of his voice startled Mary, and she looked toward the defense table. Still staring straight ahead, Ted had his elbows on the table and was silently moving his balled right fist over and over into his flat left hand. Seeing the gesture frightened Mary, and her face went pale.

Shaw saw this and looked quickly toward Ted. Judge Belfor followed his gaze and saw Ted's fist contact his flat hand twice before he realized eyes were on him, and he dropped his hands to the table.

"Your Honor, Mr. Brennen is trying to intimidate this witness," Shaw said angrily.

Before Shaw could finish the sentence, the judge pointed toward Ted.

"Mr. Brennen, if I see any other attempt to influence a witness's testimony, I will immediately rule for a trial," he said sharply. "Mr. Ryan, make sure your client knows the severity of his actions in this courtroom."

He then turned to Mary.

"Please repeat what you had to say," he instructed.

"It was Ted Brennen that was outside staring at our house," Mary said, this time with a note of defiance. The judge's sharp rebuke of Ted had done wonders for her confidence.

Shaw said he had no more questions and returned to his table.

"If I may, Your Honor?" Ryan said. Belfor motioned him to proceed.

"How many times did you see Ted staring at your house?" he asked.

"I saw him once then went to tell my mom," she answered.

"Did she see him?" Ryan asked.

"Yes," Mary answered.

"Did you see him any other time besides this one?" Ryan asked.

"No, but I'm sure it wasn't the only time," Mary said hesitantly.

"But you only saw him this one time," Ryan said more than asked.

Mary did not answer.

"One time does not constitute stalking," Ryan said as he returned to his seat.

Sherry described the events she went through in Wyoming and Carson. At times, her testimony was brief with little detail. It was at those times that Shaw prodded her with questions.

"What did you do to let Mr. Brennen know you did not want to have sex?" he asked after she told about the Wyoming rape.

"I told him no," she said.

"But that didn't stop him?" Shaw asked.

"No," Sherry said.

"So what did you do?" he asked.

"I tried to push him away," she answered.

"What was his reaction to that?" the prosecutor asked.

"He kept trying to pull down my pants," Sherry said.

Relating these intimate details was starting to wear on Sherry's resolve, and Shaw could see it happening. But he had to press on.

"I know this is difficult, Sherry, but it is important," he said. "How long did you resist?"

"Until he hit me," she said.

"And that is when the alleged rape happened?" Shaw asked. He had briefed the entire Dyke family on his use of the word *alleged* when referring to the rape. He knew Ryan would object each time if he did not, and getting that repeated objection into the record was something he wanted to avoid. Sherry was not happy about it but said she understood.

"No, I kept trying to fight back, then he hit me again. That is when he 'allegedly' raped me," Sherry said, using the first two finger on each hand like visual quote marks held up just enough so Shaw could see them over the witness stand partition. She hadn't told him she was going to do it, but when he saw it, he couldn't help but smile a little bit.

Judge Belfor, looking down into the witness box, saw the gesture as well. He quickly looked away and rested his chin in his hand with the fingers covering the smile that spread across his lips.

"When you were attacked outside Carson, what did you do to resist?" Shaw asked.

The memory brought a bit of satisfaction to Sherry's mind, knowing that what she had done hurt Ted physically. But at the same time, it brought back the pain that followed.

"When he had 'that thing' in me, I slammed my legs together, and it hurt him," she explained. "When he took it out, I kicked out at him, and I think I got him in the crotch."

"Weren't you being restrained by two other men?" Shaw asked.

"Yes, but one of them lost his grip," Sherry answered.

"So you also said you were blindfolded at the very beginning. How did you know it was Mr. Brennen who allegedly raped you?" Shaw asked.

"I recognized his voice," Sherry said.

"You had not heard his voice in more than a year, how could you be sure it was his?" Shaw asked.

"I had dated him for a while before the 'alleged' rape," Sherry said, using the visual quote marks again. "And when you are 'allegedly' raped and the 'alleged' rapist speaks, that voice is burned into your brain."

Her continued use of the visual quote marks indicated to Shaw that Sherry had moved past the uncomfortable stage in her testimony. It also indicated that she was hardening her heart. The shy, timid young girl he first met when the case started was changing, becoming more aggressive, more willing to strike out to protect herself any way she could. This was a good sign. Shaw was convinced this change would pay dividends when the case finally went to trial.

"Is there anything else that made you think your alleged attacker was Mr. Brennen?" Shaw asked.

"The handkerchief that was used to blindfold me was something I knew he had used, he was wearing red bikini underwear I knew he wore, and he was wearing work boots like they wear at the mill where he worked," Sherry explained.

"Was there anything else that helped you identify Mr. Brennen as your alleged attacker?" Shaw asked.

Sherry knew this moment was coming. Despite her growing self-confidence, it was still an uncomfortable subject to talk about. But she knew it was something she had to do.

"I could tell 'that thing' that was inside me was his," she said.

The entire courtroom heard the double gasps coming from the spectator section. Katrina and Mary had both reacted to the statement. So did Bob, but his reaction was much different.

The image of any man violating any of his daughters by sticking their dirty cocks inside them was too much for him to bear. He jumped out of his seat and moved toward the aisle. The bailiff nearest him moved forward, thinking he was headed for the defense table. But once Bob got to the aisle, he turned left and stormed out of the courtroom. He couldn't listen to it anymore; otherwise, he knew he would probably lose it.

Ralph got up and followed his father. Just as much for the same reasons but also to be there to support him and comfort him. Katrina started to follow her husband, but when Ralph went first, she settled back in her seat.

After attention turned from the commotion of the Dyke men's departure back to the courtroom, Shaw said he had no more questions, thinking that was the end of it. He was ready to rest his case.

Ryan dispelled that.

"I do have a few questions, Your Honor," he said, standing and moving toward the witness stand.

Sherry had a brief moment of panic. Shaw had not prepared her for challenges from the defense attorney to any of her testimony. It was a calculated risk on his part, mostly designed to keep her and her family's confidence high.

But as Ryan began to speak, Sherry tapped into the reserves of her resolve.

"So you had not heard Ted's voice in more than a year. Are you absolutely certain it was his?" he asked.

"As I said, that voice is burned into my brain," she answered.

Ryan smiled. She had walked into his trap.

"I have talked to psychologists who will testify at trial that when someone is traumatized, that a voice burned into the brain, as you describe it, can be the only voice you recognize in another traumatic event," Ryan said. "Do you think that is what happened in this case?"

What she thought was irrelevant to Ryan. He just wanted to get the promise of a psychological testimony into the record and possible doubt into the judge's brain.

"It was his voice I heard that night and no one else's," Sherry spat at the attorney.

"We shall see," he sneered. "So let's turn to your other method of identification," he continued. "I find it hard to believe that any woman can recognize one penis from another."

Sherry was quick with her response before Ryan could get out his next question.

"Have you ever had a man's penis inside you?" she asked with a steely-eyed look that made even her mother shiver.

Her retort caught Ryan off guard.

"No, I haven't," he answered then wondered why he had.

"Then you and your psychologist have no idea," she said, staring straight into his eyes. It made him blink.

"Then tell me, what is it about Mr. Brennen's penis that makes you able to recognize it?" Ryan asked, working hard to recover his composure.

"He was not circumcised, for one thing," she answered, still staring him down.

"There are hundreds of men out there who are not circumcised," Ryan said.

"You put them all in a room with him, blindfold me, have them talk. And I'll grab their penises, and I can tell you which one is him one hundred out of one hundred times," Sherry said angrily. While she kept her eyes locked on Ryan's, it was clear she was starting to lose her patience.

"By your own admission, Ted is the only man you've had penetrative sex with," Ryan said. "You have no means of comparison. How would you know other men's penises don't feel the same?"

"Trust me, Mr. Attorney, I would know that prick anywhere," Sherry said in a tone that made the courtroom feel like a walk-in freezer.

"I assume you are talking about his penis," Ryan said and turned toward his table.

"If you say so," Sherry answered.

Realizing that things might start to spin out of control as Ryan turned back to respond, Shaw stood at his table.

"Your Honor, if Mr. Ryan is through badgering my witness, can we go on?" he asked.

Judge Belfor looked to Ryan still standing in the middle of the room staring at Sherry sitting smugly in the witness box. He threw up his hands and said he was finished with his questioning.

"Then we will take a recess while I consider the facts in this case," the judge said. "We will reconvene in one hour."

Chapter 16

Bill Shaw took a few minutes to lead the Dyke family and Barry to a conference room.

"Wait here, and I'll come and get you when the judge lets us know the session will be back," he told them.

They all looked drained from the experience they had gone through in the courtroom. In addition, they were all a bit nervous. As Shaw had said, it didn't seem like a slam dunk or even a Rip City, as the questions from Keith Ryan were unsettling. However, Sherry hoped her time on the stand presented to the judge a picture of confident defiance.

"What do you think is going to happen?" she asked Shaw as he was heading for the door. "Did we do okay?"

Shaw stopped with his hand on the doorknob and thought for a few seconds then turned to face her.

"It is hard to say what the judge will decide," he responded, trying to hedge his bets. But seeing the disappointed looks on the other faces in the room, he went on, "But I believe we put up a very good case. And all our witnesses are very credible."

Shaw was afraid to look at Bob, but if he had, he would have seen a look of guilt on his face.

"I am confident we have a good case here to take to trial," Shaw said then gave a curt nod and left the room.

Once Shaw was gone, Bob moved to Sherry and gave her a hug.

"I'm sorry, sweetie," he said into her hair. "I might have messed things up in there."

She squeezed him tight around the waist then pulled back to look him in the eye.

"No, Dad, you didn't mess things up," she said. "You just expressed how I'm sure we all feel."

Katrina and the rest of her children joined Bob and Sherry, hugging them both in turn. After a moment, Katrina looked over at Barry, who remained at a corner of the conference table. She motioned for him to join them.

"Come on, Barry, you're part of us too," she said.

He walked over and joined the group, putting his arm around Sherry and pulling her close.

"Everything will be all right," he said. "No matter what happens from here on."

"But we all know what we want from this," Bob said. "That bastard needs to pay for what he's done, and if the court system doesn't provide that, it will have to come from somewhere."

Nearly all in the family circle, including Sherry, nodded their agreement. The only head not nodding was Katrina's.

"We can't talk like that or even think like that," she said. "We have to have faith in the system."

"It hasn't worked out so well for us so far," Ralph said.

"No, it hasn't," Katrina agreed. "But we can't just go off and take matters into our own hands."

Barry separated from the group and sat in a chair at the end of the table. He began to tremble, and anger crept across his face.

"Someone like this guy has to be dealt with in a way that he understands," he said. "He doesn't care about the system's justice. He made fun of it in there. He was like that on the bridge when I caught up with him. He's all for using the system when he thinks it will work for him, but past that, he thinks he's above the law."

Sherry sat in the chair next to him and took his hands. They stared into each other's eyes for a few moments. Slowly she could feel his trembling subside.

"I understand, Barry, I really do," she said.

The rest of the family took seats around the table, watching Sherry and Barry, who continued to be locked onto each other. Katrina was the first to speak.

"We have to have faith and confidence that the judge will make the right decisions," she said.

A full hour had passed, and the Dykes were getting antsy. Just as Bob was ready to go looking for the prosecutor, the door to the conference room opened, and he walked in, looking confident. But the family could see a touch of a crack in that confidence.

"What's happening? Where have you been?" Bob asked eagerly, tinged with a little anger.

Shaw held up his hand.

"I'm sorry that you have been waiting for so long and no one came to talk to you," he said. "The judge will reconvene in about twenty minutes."

There were sighs of relief from everyone else in the room.

"I have been meeting with Mr. Brennen's attorney, trying to get a plea change," Shaw told them.

"You mean you've been trying to make some kind of deal," Kim said.

Shaw was a little surprised that she spoke up. Someone so young understanding how the system worked was a little unexpected. But then again, there were a lot of courtroom dramas on television.

"Yes, I have," he said.

"And…?" Sherry prodded.

"My offer was to drop the attempted murder charge in exchange for guilty pleas on the other charges," he explained.

He glanced at the expectant looks on each face in the room.

"They are not interested," he said.

There was a pregnant moment of silence.

"So this will go to court?" a timid voice uttered. All eyes turned to Kim. She had not been called as a witness, but she had been in the courtroom to hear all the testimony and see the evidence presented.

In the beginning, she believed that the proceedings they were watching this day was the trial. Shaw had explained to the entire family, including her, about preliminary hearings and how that was the determination of whether a case went to a trial.

"Not quite, Kim," Shaw said. "Remember when I explained about this hearing? The judge has to decide after hearing the evidence."

"But he has heard it, and it sure seems clear to me what he did to Sherry," Kim said, almost pleading.

"It's a little more complicated than that," Shaw said. "The judge has to take everything said in there into account, including what the defense attorney said."

She shook her head. "I still don't understand. He did horrible things to my sister," she said.

Shaw could think of nothing else to say to the young girl that would help her see the system more clearly, nor could he think of anything to say to her to ease her grief. He was a court prosecutor, not a counselor. Sherry broke the awkward silence that filled the room.

"I think we're all having trouble understanding it," she said, looking around at her family. She then turned to Shaw. "But we have faith in you and the court system," she said. "Maybe we should get out to the courtroom."

With Shaw sitting at the prosecution table, the Dykes lined the benches behind him across the waist-high wooden barrier between them. They chattered in low voices in twos and threes for a few moments. Most of the talk was about the outcome they expected from the judge.

Shaw shuffled through his notes and documents, jotting down new notes here and there. He had gone straight to his position when the group entered the courtroom. As he went through the gate at the barrier, he turned and gave the Dykes a polite wave and a smile. He hoped it conveyed confidence and embedded that feeling in them.

Ted and Ryan were at the defense table when they all entered the room. Ted again sat ramrod straight in his seat staring ahead of him, stone-faced and emotionless. Like Shaw, Ryan shuffled through some papers in front of him. Unlike Shaw, he was not making notes.

When the door to the right of the judge's bench opened, all eyes were on it.

"All rise. The court is now in session. Judge Ronald Belfor presiding," the bailiff recited, as he had done hundreds of times before.

Belfor strode to his chair atop the bench and stood for a moment, surveying the courtroom and its occupants. His face was emotionless. Finally, he sat down and rapped his gavel lightly on the Portland Buckaroos hockey puck. It was less than an authoritative slap, and that gave Shaw concern.

The judge sat and stared straight ahead, motionless for a few seconds, then began to speak.

"This preliminary hearing is convened to decide whether there is enough evidence to warrant a trial for Ted Brennen on charges including rape, assault, and attempted murder," he said then paused again. "Have the respective attorneys had a chance to meet and discuss resolution prior to the conclusion of this hearing?" he asked.

"Yes, we have, Your Honor," Shaw said, standing. "The state has offered to drop the attempted murder charges in exchange for a guilty plea on all other charges."

"And the defense's response?" the judge directed toward Ryan.

The defense attorney stood quickly, a mix of defiance and fear in his eyes. He knew the next words out of his mouth would be a huge gamble.

"We reject the offer," he said then sat as quickly as he stood. He did not hazard a glance at either Shaw or his client. Ted remained just as he had been, fixated on a point on the wall in front of him.

"That is unfortunate," Belfor whispered, but loud enough for the two attorneys to hear. The remark made Shaw's heart skip a beat. But there was little time to process the moment and its ramifications. Judge Belfor launched right into his first comments on the case.

"The prosecution has proven without a shadow of a doubt that there were crimes committed, very heinous crimes," he said.

This first remark caused every member of the Dyke family and their supporters in the courtroom to sit forward in their seats with hope in their hearts.

"There is clear and believable testimony that an attack and rape were perpetrated upon the victim, Ms. Dyke," he said. "The court is inclined to believe her testimony as to the events of the night in question."

More hope was poured into the Dykes and their supporters. Shaw, however, was not as confident. He debated on whether to turn and try to give the family some sign of not to get their hopes up. But in the end, he decided not to. As he had from the beginning of his involvement with the family, he did not want to give them any indication the decision could go against them.

"There is also physical evidence that shows clearly that at least one male and up to three were involved in the criminal activities," Belfor said.

The judge paused for a moment, looked down at his notes, then back up to face the family and prosecutor. There was a sadness in his eyes when he looked up that was recognized immediately by Bob, Katrina, Sherry, and Barry.

"Oh god," Sherry whispered. Barry squeezed her hand and leaned in to touch his head to hers.

"What is missing is clear and unquestionable evidence that Mr. Brennen was even one of the attackers," the judge said and went on before anyone else could speak. "While Ms. Dyke claims the voice she heard from the main attacker was Mr. Brennen's, the defense's contention that the previous incident with Mr. Brennen could influence her recollection in another similar traumatic incident is substantiated in case law."

Shaw stood angrily.

"I object, Your Honor!" he shouted. "We could bring forward our own experts that can testify to the contrary. We want the opportunity to explore that at trial."

Now the doubt that had crept into Bob's, Katrina's, Sherry's, and Barry's minds was spreading among Ralph and Mary and the family's supporters in the room. A low murmur began to rumble among them as they whispered their oaths of dismay.

Judge Belfor smacked the hockey puck harder than they had heard so far. The sound stilled all noise in the courtroom.

GORGE JUSTICE

"There will be order in the court, or I will have it cleared," he said, not with anger but more with a touch of pity.

With so little noise in the courtroom all could hear a feather hit the tiled floor, the judge continued.

"As to the other identifying factor, I, too, have never had a man's penis inside me, so I have no way to judge whether it is possible to identify a man by the feel of his sexual organ," the judge said sheepishly. "Therefore, I cannot validate that as a clear and unquestionable identification of Mr. Brennen as the main attacker."

The judge's words were slowly starting to filter into Ted's brain, and a smug smile began to turn the corners of his mouth upward.

"The crimes committed in this case are vile and disgusting," Belfor continued. "I have a daughter, and I would be just as eager as the Dyke family to see justice done if something like this were to happen to her."

The thought of that made Belfor pause for a second before continuing. The same sadness creeped back onto his face as he continued.

"The evidence and testimony in this case is purely circumstantial," he said. "In a case such as this, where a man's very life is on the line, we must be certain we have the right person charged. With no clear and unquestionable identification, I don't believe that certainty exists."

Belfor looked at Ryan and Ted.

"Therefore, this case will not go to trial," he said. "Mr. Brennen is free to go."

Ted leaped from his seat, pumped his fist downward, and yelled, "Yes!"

Belfor rapped his gavel on the hockey puck.

"Mr. Brennen, you will control yourself in my courtroom, or I will find you in contempt," the judge admonished.

Ted sat down and waved his hand dismissively at the judge.

"And you will display the proper respect in this court," Belfor said. "If I were not a judge in this case and forced to be impartial, I would be inclined to believe Ms. Dyke's testimony concerning your involvement. As it is, you need to respect and be thankful for my impartiality."

"That's bullshit," Ted said defiantly. "You already said I didn't do anything."

The hockey puck got another smack as Ryan tried to keep his client quiet.

"No, Mr. Brennen, that was not my ruling, which was there was not enough evidence to bring this to trial," Belfor said, getting angrier. "There is a large difference."

Again, the dismissive wave from Ted, and the judge banged the hockey puck again.

"One more sign of disrespect from you, Mr. Brennen, and you will be in contempt," he said. "I have just set you free. I suggest you now take advantage of that opportunity and go on with your life… somewhere other than the Pacific Northwest."

Shaw sat at his table, shocked at the judge's remarks. They were clearly expressing his contempt for Ted and gave the prosecutor a new insight into the judge's mind. He obviously believed Sherry's account and identification of her attacker but had to go by the letter of the law. His remarks to Ted about his personal feeling about the case and suggesting Ted leave the area were statements out of the ordinary for a judge to make. He hoped he could explain that sufficiently to the Dyke family to ease their grief and anger.

Ryan was trying desperately to get his client to curb his outbursts. But Ted was having none of it.

"How dare you, you fraud!" he shouted. "You have no right to tell me where I can and cannot live my life."

The gavel banged down hard on the hockey puck, making it bounce on the bench.

"You are now in contempt!" he hollered back at Ted, hardly able to contain his anger. "You will sit in the county jail until you feel the urge to apologize to this court and everyone in attendance today for your outbursts."

The judge waved to the bailiffs to take Ted, who began a loud stream of obscenities, out of the courtroom. Belfor looked down to see a tiny crack across the face of his prized hockey puck.

Chapter 17

When the judge pronounced that the case would not go to trial, the entire Dyke family and their supporters were stunned. In fact, they were too stunned to react immediately.

Shaw turned to face them as Belfor and Ted went at each other.

"This isn't over," he told them in hopes no one would voice their anger at the judge. He could hear what was going on behind him and knew that Belfor was getting angrier each time he had to admonish Ted. If there were any other outbursts, there was no telling what the judge might do.

"We have options to pursue," he said.

It was a reach, but he hoped that at least for the next few moments, that would mollify them. But he was disappointed when Bob stood and headed for the gate leading to the nonaudience portion of the courtroom. But Katrina stood up and grabbed his arm.

"Please sit down," she whispered. "If there is a chance to put him away, we don't want to ruin it."

The look on Bob's face was one of deep anguish. He wanted justice for his daughter any way he could get it. He could see that disappearing before his eyes, and it was like having his heart ripped from his chest.

Sherry also stood and gave her father a hug.

"This isn't the time, Dad," she whispered.

Bob looked his wife and daughter in the eyes. His were now filling with tears. He hugged them both and reluctantly sat back in his seat.

All the activity in the spectator area went unnoticed by the judge, Ted, and his attorney as they were quite busy with their own drama. When Ted was escorted from the room, Shaw spoke to the judge.

"Your Honor, I wish to file a motion to quash," he said.

Ryan, still a little distracted from his client being led off for contempt of court, switched his thinking when he heard Shaw's statement.

"I object, Your Honor. This is completely irregular," he said.

Belfor, still looking at his damaged hockey puck, lifted his head to face Shaw.

"He is correct, Mr. Shaw," he said. "But just out of curiosity, under what grounds will your motion be filed?"

Shaw paused for a moment to organize his thoughts. A motion to quash is normally filed when there has been a mistake by the court or some irregularity in documents. He knew he was on shaky ground, especially since all the documents and evidence in the hearing were presented by him. How could he challenge his own documents without being laughed out of court?

"By virtue of the defendant's behavior and your own remarks," he volunteered.

"My remarks?" Belfor asked. "What remarks?"

"I heard you say that you believed Ms. Dyke's testimony," he said.

Belfor frowned. "That is not exactly what I said," he muttered then spoke in a firmer tone. "I said that it might—I repeat, might—be possible if I were not a judge in this case."

"I stand corrected, Your Honor, but I still plan to file my motion," Shaw said.

Belfor fingered the cracked hockey puck, a little distracted.

"You go ahead and file your motion, Mr. Shaw, and I will give it the consideration it deserves," Belfor said.

He then picked up the puck, rapped his gavel lighting on the bench, and turned to his left and began to walk down the three steps at the end behind the witness stand.

"Court is dismissed," he said as he left the room.

As the family left the courthouse, Sherry searched for Barry. He had left the courtroom before the rest and had not returned. But as the family stood outside the courtroom preparing to get into the station wagon, Barry came bounding out of the building and joined them at the curb.

"I'm not going back to La Grande until tomorrow," he told Sherry.

Sherry took both his hands and gave them a little squeeze.

"That's sweet, Barry, but you don't need to stay. I'll be all right," she said, looking deep into his eyes. "You'll miss your classes."

"I only have two tomorrow, and I called my roommate, Dan, and he's going to go and take notes and explain to the professors for me."

"But it's not necessary," she argued. Barry hushed her with an index finger to her lips.

"I want to be here for you," he said.

She tried to stop them, but tears filled her eyes and ran down her cheeks. She was trying to present the facade of strength to him. Barry had been there for her since before the attack, and he was always there through the aftermath. She believed he had done enough. She needed to be strong because he could not be there at all times and still pursue his education.

But when she looked at it honestly, she needed him more than ever now, even if it were just for one more day.

They hugged long and hard. When the embrace broke, Barry looked over at Bob and Katrina.

"I'll take her home," he said.

Katrina walked to him and gave him a light hug.

"Thank you for being here," she said then returned to her family. They piled into the car and drove away.

As they walked to Barry's Grand Prix, he asked Sherry if she was hungry. She answered in the affirmative, but she really wasn't. Her answer was for him because she knew he was, or he wouldn't have asked.

As they sat in a small booth at the little red diner near the Carson junction, they didn't speak for a few minutes after they ordered. Finally, Sherry broke the silence.

"I don't know if I can take any more time in court," she said. "I think we should ask Mr. Shaw to end this."

Barry took her hands in his. He paused before speaking.

"I think we should look into every option available to get that bastard what he deserves," he said.

"But I don't see that happening through the court system," she said. "He's going to get away with all this, and that makes me very frustrated and angry."

Barry understood her feelings. He felt his own frustration and anger. He loved her and wanted to protect her and keep her safe. But so much cruelty and misery was visited upon her, and he couldn't do anything to stop it. Now all he wanted to do was find a way to relieve her of her suffering.

But Barry agreed with Sherry about not getting justice from the courts.

"What that son of a bitch deserves is way past the courts," he said.

"Oh, I agree," she said. "He needs to know exactly what I went through."

"That's for sure," Barry answered. "I'd love to be the one to make sure he knows."

"So would I," Sherry said.

They looked at each other for a long moment. The waitress interrupted with their food. When she went back behind the counter, Barry and Sherry launched into a hushed discussion of just what they would do to Ted to make him feel what Sherry had gone through. But in the cramped diner, their conversation was not hushed enough to keep the waitress and three other diners from hearing.

The following day, Barry was at Sherry's home by five thirty in the morning. He had told her the day before he wanted to take her to an early breakfast before he got started back to La Grande by noon.

GORGE JUSTICE

It was only half true, as he had another plan in mind.

As with their earlier trip to Hood River and The Dalles, he wanted to give her some time away from her turbulent life and worries. He wanted their last time together until his next break from school to be as pleasant as possible.

Sherry, looking forward to some quality time with him, was ready when Barry arrived. They shared some chitchat with Bob and Katrina before setting out just before six o'clock.

Barry guided the Grand Prix down the road to the junction with State Route 14 near the little red diner. Sherry thought that was where he was going to take her for breakfast, so she was surprised when he headed west toward Stevenson. When he bypassed the town and crossed the Bridge of the Gods, she became very curious.

"Where are we going?" she asked as the car headed down the entrance ramp to westbound Interstate 80.

"You'll see," he said with a sly smile. "Just sit back and enjoy the ride."

She smiled back at him and put her left hand on his right thigh. Guiding the car with his left hand on the steering wheel, he covered her hand with his.

Just west of the small hamlet of Dodson, he got off the freeway and onto the Historic Columbia River Highway. Sherry's heart skipped a beat, and excitement warmed her entire body.

Until the freeway was completed through the Columbia Gorge in the early 1970s, the historic highway, designated US 30, was the only route through the Gorge from east to west. The seventy-five-mile stretch of highway ranged between The Dalles on the east end and Troutdale, a Portland suburb, on the west end.

Built between 1913 and 1922, the highway was promoted by lawyer and entrepreneur Sam Hill and engineer Samuel C. Lancaster to be modeled after the great scenic roads of Europe. The narrow two-lane highway includes, along much of the length, the original ornate stone guards on the river side of the roadway. Over time, they have become covered with moss, characteristic of the Pacific Northwest's year-round moist environment.

Scattered throughout the route are some of the most beautiful waterfalls, including Multnomah, Latourell, Breonta, Wahkeena, and Bridal Veil.

While Barry and Sherry's time on the freeway went quickly, the pace was slower on the old highway. That was okay with Sherry, who was enjoying the view, as much as she could see in the darkness, with the sun still not up in the east. The drive was mostly a straight shot until it passed Multnomah Falls. Following the tree line on the mountainous south bank of the river, Sherry could catch brief glimpses of the waterway.

But west of Multnomah Falls, the road began a series of switchbacks as it climbed the steep rock mountain leading to Crown Point. Sherry knew now they were headed for Vista House.

Located at the peak of Crown Point, the octagonal stone structure was built in 1917–18, designed by Edgar M. Lazarus in the art nouveau style. It was intended to give travelers along the highway a chance to stop and rest. A series of concession shops were operated within the structure under different owners through the years. But its biggest draw was an overwhelming panoramic view of the Columbia Gorge, especially looking eastward.

As Barry's Grand Prix slowly climbed the switchbacks, Sherry's excitement grew by leaps and bounds. So, too, did her feelings for Barry. She thought her love for him was at its peak. But she was wrong.

The car made the circle around Crown Point with the Vista House above to their left. When they were on the west side, Barry steered his car into the upper parking lot nearest the Vista House. Surprisingly, they were the only visitors at this hour. When they exited the car, Sherry ran over and gave Barry a tight bear hug.

"Thank you so much," she said into his ear. "This is awesome."

"Just wait," he said as he broke the embrace and led her to the stone half wall lining the driveway around the Vista House.

They were at the northeast portion of the wall facing east. Below them, they could see the highway circling the point upon which the house was constructed. Farther out, 733 feet below them, was the mighty Columbia River.

GORGE JUSTICE

Barry and Sherry stood side by side with their arms around each other. Though they both had warm jackets on, the damp breeze made the forty-degree weather seem closer to the freezing point. But they enjoyed each other's body heat, and it made it bearable. So did what came next.

Under a canopy of scattered but full clouds that extended all the way to the west behind the couple, a strip of sky to the east was starting to turn a light blue then slowly transitioned into a light orange. The Gorge laid out in front of them was still shrouded in darkness, with the river itself only distinguishable because of its calmness compared to the forests and rugged mountains on either side.

As the minutes passed and the sun made its slow crawl toward the horizon, the gray clouds began to become trimmed in a bright red. The color filled the puffy clouds as if paint were filling balloons, and the clear strip of sky took on a darker version of orange. Eventually, the upper portion of the clouds took on a purple hue.

Barry and Sherry had just marveled at the masterpiece in the sky when the sun made its first tentative peek over the eastern horizon. Suddenly, the panoramic Gorge began to light up. Off in the distance, Rooster Rock on the Washington side became fully visible, and the river's water exposed its bright blue color.

Sherry's eyes were transfixed on the sunrise from the time they stood at the wall. But Barry snuck a few peeks at her. Each time, he beamed a wide smile to see her so enthralled in nature's beautiful work.

When the sun was fully above the rim of the earth, the clouds had become a kaleidoscope of pinks, reds, oranges, blues, and purples. The Gorge below was now fully lit, adding the greens, yellows, and browns of fall.

After a few moments, the sky colors began to fade, and the sun was steadily heading toward the gray cloud cover. Finally, Sherry turned to face Barry. He saw tears in her eyes, but the smile on her face told him they were tears of joy.

"This was my gift to you," he said, motioning toward the eastern sky.

"Thank you," she choked out then threw her arms around him and squeezed him as tightly as she could.

"Now let's get out of the cold and have some breakfast," Barry said.

Throughout the morning, not a word was said about Ted, their conversation from the previous day, or Sherry's ordeal. It was exactly what Barry had wanted for her, to take her away from it all, even if only for a few hours.

Despite that, once they had eaten breakfast and Barry began the drive back to La Grande, their conversation in the diner the previous day returned to both their minds.

At the end of the Monday preliminary hearing, after Ted had gotten himself thrown in jail again for contempt of court, Bob asked the prosecutor how he could find out when Ted was released again. Shaw assured him he would call when that occurred.

He was true to his word. When the courthouse closed for the day on Monday, Tuesday, and Wednesday, Bob received a call that let him know that Ted was still incarcerated.

Bob had been at the mill two hours on Thursday when at about eight thirty in the morning, he saw Larry Cartwright waving frantically at him from the mill office. Bob had just finished checking each station in the log cutting process, so he jogged to the office door.

"There is a phone call for you," Larry said loudly to be heard over the din of heavy machinery, conveyors, and buzzing saws around them. "It's from the courthouse."

Bob felt his heart quicken, but he slipped past Larry and picked up the receiver from where it lay on the desk.

"Hello," he blurted out nervously.

"This is Bill Shaw," the voice on the phone said. "Something's happening."

* * *

Ted sat in the holding cell at the Skamania County Courthouse for three nights and two full days. Other inmates came and went as they were transferred to courtrooms and back or to other jurisdictions. But Ted was the only constant from Monday night to Thursday morning.

Each day, his court-appointed public defender paid him a visit to see whether he was ready to apologize to the judge and regain his freedom. Each day, Ted refused in ever-increasing defiant tones. But when he was back in the holding cell, his irrational resolve slowly started to crack.

Ted Brennen was a stubborn man. Some would apply another word that started with *S*. There were other words that started with other letters of the alphabet. There was also a heavy dose of arrogance in his personality. He called it confidence.

But for all the trouble his personality brought him, this was the first time he had spent any time in jail. And after several months of it, the experience was leaving a sour taste in his mouth.

So when Keith Ryan showed up at the jail at seven o'clock in the morning on Thursday for his daily check-in to see if his client was ready to offer his apologies to the judge, Ted was in a more receptive mood. But he just could not help himself. It was in his nature.

"Hell no, I won't apologize to that pompous ass," he spat. "He had no right to lecture me after he said I was free to go."

But Ryan was in a foul mood. On Monday, he had reveled in his win in court over the veteran prosecutor. That good feeling didn't last more than a few seconds, though, as his client went off the deep end and got himself sent back to jail right after being declared a free man.

Shaw's congratulatory handshake later was sincere, but Ryan already knew the victory was tainted. In the days that followed, it became more so as the whisperings behind his back made their way to him through the courthouse grapevine. He had already grown tired of the daily visits to a client who did not know what was good for him. He went into the visiting area on Thursday, ready to get the apology the judge required or walk away.

"I'm tired of repeating myself and ending up just banging my head against a brick wall," he told Ted. "This judge is ready to let you rot in here if he doesn't get what he wants."

Ted thought about that for a few seconds before responding.

"So you think I should grovel?" he said.

"If you want to be a free man, yes," Ryan said peevishly.

"So what would I have to say?" Ted asked.

Feeling like he was finally putting a crack in that brick wall, Ryan softened his tone a bit.

"You should just say you apologize for your outburst in court and ask for the mercy of the court," Ryan said.

"And that's it, no more lectures?" Ted asked.

Ryan saw the crack in the brick wall disappear as if it were filling with silicone.

"Mr. Brennen, do you want out of jail or do you want to take up permanent residence here?" Ryan shouted, banging a fist on the table between them. The unexpected action startled Ted, and he visibly jumped in his chair.

"I want out, but if there's going to be no trial, I shouldn't be treated like I'm guilty," Ted said, the defiance in his voice a bit muted.

Ryan recognized the opportunity but, at the same time, knew his patience had come to an end.

"Mr. Brennen, you need to understand the seriousness of your situation," he said as professionally and matter-of-factly as he could. "There is a great deal of circumstantial evidence that points to you as the person responsible for the victim's injuries."

Ted began to speak, but Ryan silenced him with an angry look and the palm of his hand.

"Judge Belfor had no choice to rule the way he did because circumstantial cases rarely hold up in court. He didn't want to waste time and taxpayer money," Ryan went on. "If the police or prosecutors find anything—and I mean even the thinnest shred—that ties you to this, you'll be right back in court and likely headed for a trial."

Ryan took a breath and studied his client, who remained silent.

"Hell, I don't even believe what you have told me," Ryan blurted out. It hadn't been planned but was more a function of his frustration with Ted. "I believe you were involved."

"So why are you my lawyer?" Ted asked sarcastically.

Ryan noted that Ted had not denied any involvement.

"Because everyone deserves to be defended, and I was assigned to your case," he said. "If this does come back to the court and you need a public defender and I get assigned, I will recuse myself."

"What the hell does that mean?" Ted asked.

"That means, you dumbass, that I will refuse to be your lawyer."

Ted seemed a little pained rather than angry at Ryan's reference to his intelligence.

"All right, I'll apologize," Ted said sheepishly.

Chapter 18

Bob hung up the phone in the mill office and turned to Larry, who had stepped inside and waited. There was a look of urgency on Bob's face.

"Can you cover for me for a couple of hours?" he asked.

"Sure. What's up?" Larry responded immediately.

"That bastard Brennen is going to court this morning, and he might end up getting out of jail. I want to be there for that."

"Go," Larry said. "I'll clear it with the boss."

Bob ran out to the mill's utility pickup truck he used around the yard and to run errands into town when needed. He fired up the engine and gunned it toward State Route 14. Squealing onto the blacktop, he headed west.

Minutes later, he rolled up to the little red diner, jumped out, and went inside to find Katrina serving a plate of pancakes to a customer at the counter.

"We've got to go to Stevenson," he told her.

Katrina gave him a puzzled look, then the realization came to her.

"Is he out?" she asked.

"I think he will be," Bob answered.

GORGE JUSTICE

Katrina looked through the service window that separated the dining area from the small kitchen. Duane Masters, the cook and owner, gave her a nod. He knew the situation well.

"Go ahead. I'll have Linda come in to cover," he said.

She untied her short apron and dropped it on the shelf on her side of the counter. She told Duane thank you as she rounded the counter and joined her husband. She and Bob left the building and climbed into the truck. Bob was careful about pulling out of the gravel parking lot but gunned the truck's engine once they were on the highway.

Bob and Katrina opened the door to the courtroom and saw Bill Shaw setting up his paperwork at the prosecution table. Keith Ryan was already seated at the defense table opposite. They both turned to see who had come in. Ryan quickly turned back to the papers in front of him. Shaw walked slowly toward the couple.

"Bob, I said there was no reason for you to be here," he said. "I was just letting you know, as you requested."

"This is something we have a right to see," Katrina said before her husband could answer.

"All right, but I need to remind you that the judge will not tolerate any problems," Shaw said. "You could end up where Mr. Brennen is."

He was addressing them both, but his gaze was on Bob the whole time.

"We understand," Katrina said, squeezing Bob's hand. "We will keep quiet."

Shaw nodded and gestured for them to take their seats behind him in the first row of bench seats. He then returned to his table and sat down.

Only a few minutes later, bailiffs escorted Ted into the courtroom and led him to the other chair at the defense table. He saw Bob and Katrina sitting in the front row and scowled. But after he sat down, he did not look in their direction for some time.

Then a bailiff announced court was in session, and Judge Belfor entered and took his seat on the bench. He glanced past Shaw to see the Dykes sitting in the front row.

"Are we ready to proceed?" the judge asked. Both attorneys answered in the affirmative.

"Mr. Brennen, would you like to address the court?" Belfor asked.

Ted took a deep breath then stood up.

"Yes," he said then added after Ryan poked his leg with his finger, "yes, Your Honor."

"Proceed," Belfor said.

"I apologize to you and the court for the way I acted last Monday," Ted said in measured, clearly practiced tones. "I ask for the mercy of the court."

The judge could tell the words were not Ted's, most likely provided by his lawyer, and he doubted their sincerity. But he had to accept them as spoken.

"Thank you, Mr. Brennen. That was a smart choice on your part," the judge said. "But before I render my decision on this contempt charge, I have a few more things to say."

Ted started to sit down, and Ryan could see he was about to say something. He poked his client in the leg again and motioned for him to remain standing.

"Mr. Brennen, do you recall my advice to you Monday following my decision that this case would not go to trial?" Belfor asked.

"That I should leave the area," Ted said. Ryan looked up to see his client was clenching his teeth.

"That is correct," the judge said. "Of course, that is not the order of the court, nor do we have the authority to force you to do that. It is simply friendly advice."

Ted said nothing, but the judge could read the contempt on his face. Unfortunately, the court also had no authority to find someone in contempt based solely on the look on their face.

"I trust your attorney has impressed upon you how closely this case came to going to trial," Belfor said.

"Yes, he did," Ted said. Ryan poked his leg again, but Ted swatted the hand away.

"All right then, I dismiss the contempt charge, and you are now a free man...again," the judge said, hitting a new Portland Buckaroos hockey puck.

"Do you have any further business with this court?" the judge asked.

"No, Your Honor," Ryan said before Ted could speak.

"Then we stand in recess for ten minutes," the judge said, rapping his gavel again. He stood, as did everyone else, and left the room.

As the exit door closed behind the judge, Ted turned his head and looked at Bob and Katrina, and a wicked smile spread across his face. Bob jumped up, but Katrina grabbed his arm and nearly dragged him out of the courtroom.

It was a very quiet and somber family dinner at the Dyke house. Depression and anger were as thick in the air as an early morning Gorge fog.

As Katrina had dragged Bob out of the courtroom, he tried several times to turn back and attack Ted right there. But she had tightened her grip each time and pulled him more forcefully toward the door. When they were outside next to the car, she looked him deep in the yes.

"You need to calm down," she said softly. "As much as you want to, beating the crap out of him isn't going to change anything, and it will get you taken away from us when we need you the most."

Her calm, soft tone of voice did more to diminish his anger than the words she spoke.

"I don't want to beat the crap out of him. I want to kill him," Bob blurted out, tears forming in his eyes.

Katrina looked around them. There were several people nearby, walking away from and to the courthouse. A couple of heads turned their way at Bob's statement.

"You need to get past that, for your family's sake," Katrina said, the picture of calm, though inside her heart was breaking.

Bob took her in his arms and squeezed her to him.

"I know, but it's so hard," he whispered into her ear. "The things he's done to our daughter and the rest of us."

Katrina could feel a lump traveling up her throat. But she did not want to let out the scream and cry that would follow. She had to be strong, because at the moment, her husband was not. So she forced the lump back down into her churning stomach.

"We'll get through this together," she said. "Just as we always have."

Bob then drove her back to the little red diner. They kissed in the parking lot, then he went back to the mill to finish his day. The mill superintendent offered to let him take the rest of the day off. But Bob opted to work. Without Katrina there to be his rock, work was the one thing that kept him occupied enough to stop thinking about how much he wanted to wring Ted Brennen's neck and watch the life drain out of him.

When he did go home, he found Katrina and Sherry the only ones home. Katrina had told Sherry about what happened in court.

"Why didn't you come and get me so I could be there?" she asked her mother angrily.

"There wasn't time," Katrina told her. "We barely got there in time."

That seemed to satisfy her on that aspect, but then her anger turned to the justice system.

"There is no justice in this world, Mom!" she yelled then ran up the stairs to her room.

Bob and Katrina caught each of the other children as they came in the house at various times and kept them downstairs until they were all there. They then broke the news that Ted had been set free. Not a word was spoken by any of them, but the parents could read the frustration, anger, and sympathy for their sister in all their faces.

Later that night, when they knew he was off duty, they called Terry to inform him as well.

"I can take some leave and go home if you need me to," he said.

"That won't be necessary," his mother told him. "But thank you for offering."

She could hear the anguish in her eldest son's voice when he spoke again.

"In reality, Mom, all I want to do is go down there, find that bastard, and give him what he gave Sherry," he said. "He doesn't deserve to be running around free."

Katrina could understand where her son was coming from. He had heard the same from her husband and from Sherry herself. But as with Bob, she had to be the voice of reason with her son.

"Terry, that is not going to solve anything," she said. "We just need to get past it all and continue on with our lives."

She hoped Terry could not read in her voice that she was just saying what she believed she needed to keep the family calm and in control. What she really wanted was to find some way to avoid any more turmoil in her family.

Following dinner, Bob and Katrina left the house to go for a walk. The rest of the children, except Sherry, went to their rooms. She remained downstairs at the wall phone in the kitchen. She dialed the number for Barry's residence hall and asked the student receptionist to fetch him to the phone for an emergency call.

"Hello," she heard Barry's voice after a few minutes.

"It's me," Sherry said. "Ted is out of jail."

"I'm not surprised," he said with a little relief in his voice. When he was told it was an emergency call, he was afraid something had happened to Sherry.

"I am surprised that it took him this long to figure out how to get out," Barry continued. "Were you there when he went back to apologize?"

"No, Mom and Dad went but didn't tell me until after," Sherry said, still a little perturbed at her parents for keeping her from attending the court appearance. "They said there wasn't enough time to get me before they went."

"How did they know it was happening?" he asked.

"They said Mr. Shaw called Dad at the mill about an hour or so before it happened," Sherry explained.

Barry could see why Bob and Katrina would not have had time to go get or even tell Sherry about the situation. But he wasn't going to say anything to her to avoid an argument.

"How are you doing?" he asked.

She avoided the question.

"Can you come home this weekend?" she asked instead.

"I can," he answered hesitantly. The thought of seeing her again was very appealing, but making a second trip within a week was not within his budget.

"Will you?" she asked with just a tinge of anger in her tome.

"I can leave Friday afternoon," he said while mentally reworking his schedule.

"Do you remember what we talked about at the diner?" Sherry asked.

Barry thought back to the last time they were at the diner, the morning they had gone to Crown Point to watch the sunrise. They had talked about several general subjects. But he had a feeling what she was referring to.

"You mean about Ted?" he asked, grabbing the phone cradle and keeping the receiver to his ear, taking it to a bench several feet from the reception desk of the dorm. The cord from the cradle to the desk was just long enough. With the subject they were about to rediscuss, he wanted to avoid any prying ears.

"Exactly," she said. "We need to do it as soon as possible."

Barry tried to replay their conversation back in his mind. They had talked in detail about what they both would do to him if they had the chance. They each wanted him to understand the pain and violence he had put Sherry through. While each of their plans was similar, there were differences—minor ones.

However, Barry's take on the conversation was a little different than Sherry's; he was beginning to see now. He had been engaging in fantasy, venting, blowing off steam. But it was clear now that she was forming a real plan.

Barry was a little uneasy. He was ready to do anything within reason for Sherry. But what she had in mind was so extreme there was certainly risks for them both.

He decided to play along and hope he could find a way of talking her out of her plan.

"When do you want to do this?" he asked.

"If you're not here early enough Friday, we can do it on Saturday," she said.

"Is he still hanging around?" Barry asked. "I remember the judge telling him he should leave the area."

"I'll check it out tomorrow before you get here," Sherry said.

"Okay, but I'll try to get there early enough so we can talk about this some more," Barry said.

"There's nothing to talk about, Barry," she said, the anger rising in her voice. "We've talked about what we're going to do. I have everything we need, and it's now just a matter of doing it."

"I just think we should talk about this a little more so we are sure of what we are going to do," he said.

There was silence on the other end of the phone for a few moments. Then he heard a heavy sigh.

"Are you thinking you can talk me out of this?" she asked in a cold tone he had never heard from her before. "Because you'd be wasting your breath. That bastard is going to pay one way or another."

"Sherry, I'm not trying to talk you out of anything," Barry said uneasily. "I just want us to be sure of what we are doing."

Again, a few moments of silence.

"Well, I know what I'm doing," she said. "And if you're not willing to help me, I'll do it myself."

He heard the phone receiver on her end get slammed onto its receiver. He called the number again, twice, but each time got no answer.

* * *

Bob and Katrina taking a walk together was not unusual. They did it often, sometimes just the two of them and sometimes with some or all the children. This time, it was just the two of them for a reason.

While Katrina had been able to calm Bob in front of the courthouse, by the time he came home from work, his rage had built up again. She could tell this was going to be an ongoing battle.

While they walked along the streets in Carson, she kept a steady conversation going. She was careful to pick subjects that had nothing to do with the turmoil the family had gone through the last few years. She talked about times when they were younger, the adventures they had enjoyed together, the children's activities at school, their plans for the upcoming holidays.

Bob was a willing conversationalist throughout their time out of the house. He, too, wanted to remove himself from the ugliness that surrounded their family. He knew what Katrina was doing, and it just deepened his love for her. This walk was yet another confirmation that he had found the best woman in the world for him.

By the time they returned to the house, they were both laughing and joking. It was dark out, and the sky was clear enough to see the stars. Carson was a small enough town that there were no streetlights, so the stars in the black sky were strikingly clear, like pinpricks in a black velvet curtain. The couple stood in their front yard and admired them silently for about ten minutes.

When they finally went indoors, they found the first story was empty of people. The children were all upstairs. They found Kim and Mary asleep, Ralph was finishing up a paper for school, and Sherry was lying in her bed, still awake but lost in thought.

Bob and Katrina in turn bid Sherry and Ralph a good night and retired to their own room. Once inside with the door shut, they embraced. Katrina ran her hands lightly up and down his back while gingerly kissing his neck. He responded enthusiastically by caressing her back and sides, enjoying the curves that were not quite as pronounced as they used to be but still sexy and alluring.

Katrina began unbuttoning his flannel work shirt then opening it. She then dropped her hands to his belt and began to unbuckle it. She unbuttoned his jeans then began pulling him toward the adjoining master bathroom. They undressed in silence.

Each with a wet, warm washcloth, they cleaned each other from head to toe. After toweling off, they adjourned to the king-size bed and, using their hands, lips, and tongues, explored each other's bodies. Finally, Bob entered her, and they conducted a rhythmic dance of in and out that increased in pace with every stroke.

Bob and Katrina used to be loud lovemakers. But as they brought children into their lives, they learned to express themselves in different quieter ways. So the only sound in the room was the whispered moans between them.

When they climaxed, it was together. It was the first time that had happened in quite some time. That added to their ecstasy, and it took all the self-control they had to keep from returning to the full-voice screams of joy they used to belt out in those long gone younger days.

After lying side by side facing each other for a few moments, Bob stroking her still ample breasts and Katrina cooing with delight, she rolled over and went to the bathroom to clean up. Bob intended to do the same when she was done, but when she came out of the bathroom with her night shirt on, he was snoring like a lumberjack running a chainsaw.

She knew then that he would sleep soundly through the night.

Chapter 19

Ted Brennen had a busy Thursday following his release from the Skamania County Jail.

The first order of business was to find a way to get from Stevenson to his apartment in Home Valley. Since the incident on the Bridge of the Gods, his Mustang resided in the county's impound lot. When he crashed through the toll barrier and collided with the Oregon State Police car, the resulting damage rendered his car undrivable. While it sat idle in the impound lot and its owner in jail, no repairs had been done on it.

Ted arranged to have the car towed to a local body shop. The damage was repairable, but the work would take more than a week. Now he had to figure out how to pay for it when it was completed.

When he came to Washington, he brought enough cash to get by on for a month, giving him time to find a job. He worked a number of temporary jobs until he was able to get on permanently at a mill on the Oregon side of the river just about a month before his attack on Sherry. Once he found employment at the sawmill, he was able to support himself. Yes, he had a sizable bank account back in Wyoming, but it was in a local bank, not a national chain with branches everywhere.

When he got into the motel apartment in Home Valley, he was able to save up enough in the first three months to pay his rent for six months. He did the same just before going to jail in the spring, so he still had a place to live.

Getting transportation back there proved to be a challenge. There were two rental car locations in Stevenson, but neither would rent a vehicle without a credit card. But Ted found a small used car lot with a limited inventory. He was able to find a 1952 DeSoto Diplomat the owner offered for $300. The paint had peeled so much and there was so much rust it was hard to tell it had once been light blue. But it ran, and the owner assured Ted there were no major mechanical problems.

Beggars can't be choosers, so Ted had to make the deal if he wanted to get anywhere. However, all he had access to that day was $100, but he convinced the car lot owner he would have the rest the next day once he was able to get back to his apartment where he said he had more cash.

The car lot owner had his doubts he'd see the rest of the money. But he happily counted out what his customer claimed was his last $100. The DeSoto had been on the lot for two years, and he could count on one hand the number of people who had expressed interest in it. And that counted the rube he'd just sold it to.

As he drove toward Home Valley, Ted discovered the old car had very little get up and go. He could only coax it to forty miles per hour. So wherever he planned to go, he wasn't going to get there very fast.

He was starving since he had not eaten breakfast that morning. He flirted with the idea of stopping at the little red diner for a meal, but in his time before spending months in the county jail, he learned that Sherry's mother worked there. As much as he might have wanted to stick it to that family, he was smart enough and in control of his impulses enough to realize if he provoked any kind of confrontation with the Dykes, there was a good chance he would end up back in jail. That did not suit him at all.

So he stopped at the gas station in Home Valley and bought a bag of chips, several candy bars, and a can of soda to hold him over. He then drove to the mill where he had been employed to see about returning to work.

"I'm afraid you are not working here anymore," the foreman told him as they stood in the mill office. He handed Ted a sealed envelope. "Here is your last paycheck and your W2."

"What the fuck?" Ted asked. "I'm ready to go back to work. I'm not going to trial, and the charges are dropped."

"And we were ready to put you back to work Tuesday," the foreman said. "But you didn't show up, and we found out you had gone right back to jail."

"That sucks!" Ted yelled. "I need a job."

The foreman sat down at the desk and shrugged.

"Feel free to go find one," he said. "It just won't be here."

Ted's anger welled up inside him. He could feel an explosion coming. But like with the little red diner, he knew he could not afford a confrontation with anyone if he wanted to stay out of jail.

"Well, fuck you," he said as he turned for the door.

"Yeah, I know, and the horse I rode in on," Ted heard the foreman say as the door slammed shut.

For the next few hours, while there was still light in the sky, Ted made a slow tour of State Route 14 back into Stevenson and back to Home Valley, stopping at each business he thought he might find employment.

But by the time he had gotten back to his motel room apartment, he had only two slim possibilities.

That left him with few options. He sat in his two-room apartment munching the rest of the chips and sipping beers from a six-pack he bought upon his return.

With no job, he would soon deplete the last cash he had available to him. He had not set up a bank account when he came to Washington and made all his transactions in cash. Since he had paid for his apartment in two half-year chunks and had not worked for months, he only had the $427 he had stashed in his sock drawer. That would not be enough unless he was able to get a job the next day and start earning a paycheck. His rent was due again in a week.

As he drained one can of beer after another, he ran all that information through his mind over and over again. Trouble was, each time he reviewed it and tried to come up with options that kept him in Washington, he kept coming up with fewer options.

Ted Brennen did not take well to being bested by anyone. He especially did not like being outmatched by a woman. Sherry Dyke had now done it twice.

He did not like the fact that she had refused his advances in Wyoming. But his bruised ego was soothed a bit when he found out she was pregnant then was crushed again when he learned she had an abortion. Not that he was disappointed that the prospect of being a father was taken away from him. He considered her pregnancy as punishment for rejecting him sexually.

By taking her and raping her in the meadow, Ted felt he was getting even. But when she fought back, his anger got the best of him, and he inflicted as much pain on her as he could. When the police came to his door to question him about the incident, instead of playing it cool, he bolted and, in doing so, pointed the finger at himself.

But in his mind, nothing was his own fault. It was her fault he had been arrested and jailed.

Now that he was rolling it all over in his mind, he realized he would need to take the judge's decision to not send his case to trial as his final victory over Sherry Dyke. Not that he realized that he had been wrong all along. No, Ted Brennen would not admit that.

However, he was forced to admit that he had come to the end of his quest to get the better of her. As he poured the final bit of the last beer down his throat, he decided he needed to go back to Wyoming. He was sure he would find a job there, and he could get back on track with his life. There would be plenty of others like Sherry Dyke to conquer.

He packed up his small collection of clothing and other belongings into his duffel bag, took it to the DeSoto, and put it in the trunk. He went back into the apartment and wrote a note to the motel owner saying he was leaving and would not be back.

He walked unsteadily, as the beer had given him a heavy buzz, to the motel office, which was closed at this late hour, and dropped his note in the night key slot. Turning back toward his room, he thought he saw a dark figure walking east along the highway.

"Little late for someone to be hitchhiking," he muttered to himself as he opened the door to his apartment and entered.

When he made the decision to go back to Wyoming, Ted's intent was to get in the DeSoto right away and start the trip. He would drive until he could feel sleep starting to overtake him then find the next rest area and pull over for the night.

But in making his plans on the fly under the beer buzz, he had forgotten the Mustang. He wasn't ready to give up his car. So he started to rethink his plans. He also realized that starting out that night under the effects of the alcohol would not be the smartest idea.

He decided to wait until first thing in the morning to begin the journey.

Ted also had an idea about how to get his car back. He picked up the telephone receiver and dialed the number of one of his accomplices in the meadow rape.

"Kenny? This is Ted," he said when the phone was answered.

"Yeah, what do you want?" Kenny answered with a touch of suspicion in his voice.

"I'm going to be heading back to Wyoming in the morning, and I need to see if you will do me a favor," Ted said.

"If it has something to do with that chick we messed up, you can forget it," Kenny said. "I don't want to get mixed up in that again."

"That's not it," Ted said.

He then asked if Kenny knew of the body shop where he had left the Mustang. Kenny said he knew it and had done business there himself from time to time.

"My Mustang is there and is getting fixed," Ted said. "But I'm heading back to Wyoming in the morning."

"Okay, so what's the favor?" Kenny asked.

"I want you to check on it every few days and see how soon it will be ready," Ted said. "I'm going to come back in about a week to get it, but if it's ready sooner, I need you to talk to the owner and make arrangements to have him park it for me until I get back."

"I can do that," Kenny said. "How do I get ahold of you?"

"I'll have to call you when I get to Wyoming to let you know what phone number I will be at," Ted said.

"All right," Kenny said.

"Thanks, I appreciate it," Ted responded then hung up.

Now that he was going nowhere that night, he went to the small refrigerator in the apartment to get one more beer before he went to bed for the night. But when he opened the door, he saw that there was no beer there.

"That's right. I drank the last one," he muttered aloud to himself.

But he wasn't satisfied with going to bed without one more. So he went out the front door and went to the DeSoto. He had put his remaining cash in his duffel bag but needed a few dollars to get more beer.

He pushed the key into the trunk lock and turned it. The lid popped open, and he pushed it upward. He bent down to open the bag pocket where his cash was stored, pulled out a five-dollar bill, and stood up.

Just as he got fully erect, he felt the hard blow to the side of his head just above his right ear, and it knocked him forward. He smacked his forehead on the inside of the trunk lid and slumped his upper body into the trunk itself. His vision was blurred, and specks of light firing like a Fourth of July aerial display filled his eyes. He started to lift his head but felt a second blow to the head, this time square in the back just above his neck. The fireworks display in his eyes became more intense.

Ted turned his head to the left, trying to get a glimpse of what or who was behind him. His vision was still blurred, and the sparkles continued to fire off in his field of vision. But he could make out a figure that looked like a shadow.

He then noticed the shadow reaching out with a hand. In it was a red-and-white blob. He felt it being forced into his mouth. The wad smelled pungent and sweet as it passed under his nose. He had a gag reflex as it entered his mouth, as much from the smell as the cloth plugging his airway. He was forced to breathe through his nose.

Ted then felt something cover his mouth and being tied at the back of his neck. Suddenly, he could feel himself losing consciousness. Before he was completely out, he felt his body shoved into the trunk of the car and he heard the truck slam shut as the world faded to black.

Chapter 20

Ted jolted awake, his eyes opening wide. His vision was blurred; however, his sense of smell was not. His nostrils were assaulted by the sharp smell of ammonia. He could feel his heart beating as if someone were inside his chest, knocking on his rib cage. His body felt overly warm, which was surprising, as his sight cleared quickly and he could see that he was outdoors.

He was sitting with his legs out in front of him, and he could feel a tree against his back. He tried to bring his hands up to his face to wipe the film from his eyes to clear his vision. But they would not respond. He realized his hands were tied behind him. They were tied so tightly he could not even separate his hands from each other.

As he regained his full sight, Ted started to take further stock of himself and his surroundings. While the waded cloth was no longer in his mouth, he still had a strip of cloth stretched across it with the strip tied tightly behind his head.

Swiveling his head slowly from one side to the other, he saw that he was in a small clearing surrounded by tall trees. There was a small break in the trees to his right, and he could see the two ruts of a dirt road beyond. He also saw the DeSoto parked on the road to the right of the break in the trees.

As he slowly panned his head to the left, the clearing seemed to be familiar. He had been here before, but when? And why? As he continued to turn his head, he saw what looked like an old firepit. To the left of that was a rocky area.

Suddenly, there was recognition. He had been here before with two other men…and Sherry.

He was confused. Why was he here? How had he gotten here? Was this some kind of tortured dream inspired by the beer he had consumed?

As he stared at the rocky area, he was suddenly aware of a dark figure squatting next to him on the right. In the dark, he had not noticed it. The shadowy figure was dressed in all black from head to foot. Because the figure was squatting so close to him, Ted could make out the ski mask looked brand-new but the sweatshirt was a bit faded, looking more like the charred remains of a log in a campfire. The pants were also a bit faded, but he could tell they were jeans. The pants fit a bit loosely.

Upon closer inspection, he noticed there were two items that were not black at all, but it was hard to notice at first glance in the darkness of the clearing, lit only by the thousands of pinpricks of light in the night sky. The figure wore a dark-brown pair of work boots, like he had seen on many of the mill workers. The figure's hands were covered by dark-brown gloves, also similar to ones he had seen on mill workers.

In the figure's left hand was a broken capsule of smelling salts.

"Who the fuck are you, and what do you want?" Ted spat defiantly, the words slightly muffled through the gag tied through his mouth and around his head, but recognizable.

There was no answer from the shadow, but it slowly stuffed the smelling salt capsule into a pocket of the jeans. It then reached down and picked up what looked like a short, thin pole and touched it to Ted's belly. He suddenly felt a sharp, painful sensation where the pole touched his covered midsection. The pain continued for a few seconds and then stopped as the pole was pulled away. Ted slumped a little as the pain subsided to a tingle as if bugs were crawling across his belly.

"What the fuck was that?" he muttered when the tingling had stopped. The pole touched his belly again, and the pain returned then stopped after a few seconds. He sagged again, waiting for the tingling to subside. This time, he kept quiet.

The shadow stood and walked behind him. He felt its arms circle under his armpits and start to lift him up. He resisted, but he felt the toe of a work boot slam into his left side, and he relented, letting the shadow drag him to his feet.

Once erect, Ted started to make a dash for the road. But in trying to take that first step, his foot refused to move forward. With the momentum of his body pushing forward, he lost his balance and started to pitch forward, but then he felt his motion suddenly stop with his arms, tied at the wrist, yanking his shoulders back so hard it seemed they would pop out of their sockets.

The shadow was suddenly in front of him. He felt the pole jab into his belly again, and he was jolted by the pain again for a second or two. He went weak in the knees and started to bend them to drop to the ground, but the shadow thrust the pole into his belly again, this time at an upward angle, and the pain shot through him again. He stood straight up, but he could feel his knees shaking.

"Why are you doing this to me?" Ted asked with a quiver in his voice. Despite his surroundings, he could not understand who would want to inflict such pain on him and why. "Tell me what this is about."

The only answer he got from the shadow was to hold the pole up in front of his face. Now he could see two short pieces of metal extending from the end of it. Recognition suddenly filled his mind. He had seen these used on ranches and at rodeos in Wyoming to get stubborn animals to move along.

"A cattle prod," he whispered. He now knew that any act of defiance would bring the pain of the prod. While he knew it was not lethal, he also now knew from firsthand experience that it was far from pleasant. He vowed to be a bit more cooperative, at least until he could find a way to get the upper hand.

The shadow put the cattle prod on the ground and then began unbuckling Ted's belt. It then undid the button on his jeans and pulled the zipper down. A thought ran through Ted's brain.

"So this is all about giving me a blowjob?" he said sarcastically.

The shadow's head turned upward, the eyes through the only holes in the pullover mask taking a long look at him. He could see satisfaction, maybe even delight, reflected in those eyes. But he wildly misinterpreted the reason for that look.

Ted felt his jeans and underwear being yanked down simultaneously. The motion continued until they were balled up around his ankles. The shadow then picked up the cattle prod and lowered it to waist level. He suddenly realized his interpretation error and regretted his flippant remark.

"No, please," he whimpered.

But then he felt the two tongs on the cattle prod pass on either side of his exposed penis. The uncircumcised bulk made it a tight fit. But the shadow pushed on the pole until it squeezed his dick tightly and the ends of the tongs touched each of his testicles.

"You can't do this to me," he almost screamed through the gag.

There was a moment when his eyes met the shadow's. He saw that same satisfaction, but this time mixed with anger and torment. Then the shadow hit the prod's trigger.

Unlike his belly, which was not quite as sensitive and had been covered by his sweatshirt, his cock and balls had many more nerve endings, and they were exposed to the bare metal of the prod's tongs. That made for a more electrifying experience for Ted, but not in a good way.

He felt the fingers of the electricity encircle his organ and gonads and squeeze as if they were in a vice on a tool bench. The shadow kept the prod there and working, despite Ted's jerky movements to avoid the pain, for much longer than it had on the multiple shots to his belly. To Ted, it seemed like a lifetime, but it was only about thirty seconds.

The squeezing sensation in his privates continued after the current was stopped, almost as long as the prod had operated. He felt a bit of spittle work its way out of the corner of his mouth and roll slowly down his chin. As time passed, the pain and tingling subsided and finally stopped. But he could still feel the prod tongs pinning his penis and the tong points on his testicles.

GORGE JUSTICE

He could swear he saw a smile in the shadow's eyes a split second before the prod jolted to life again and the electrical squeezing began anew. When it stopped, he started to sway at the knees, and the prod sent another elongated jolt through his groin. He could see the clearing beginning to spin, and he became dizzy. He hardly noticed the prod stop shooting its load into his nether regions as he lapsed into unconsciousness again.

Ted was again jolted awake by the ammonia vapor from the smelling salts. He found that he was in a different position than he was when this all started.

Now he was lying on his belly with his arms extended past his head. His wrists were still tied together, and when he tried to pull his arms toward his body, he discovered he could only move them an inch or two. His face was turned to the right, and he saw the shadow standing up from where it had squatted to wave the smelling salt capsule under his nose.

He turned his head to face the ground then rotated his head upward so he could see his tied hands. He could see that his tied wrists were connected to a rope that went around the trunk of a tree.

As he began to regain more of his senses, Ted realized he was lying flat on the ground. He felt jabs of pain thrust into his midsection with each slight movement as the inside of his sweatshirt rubbed against the wounds caused by the application of the cattle prod there. He stopped squirming and tried to lie as still as possible.

He then noticed that his butt cheeks and legs were cold. His pants and underwear were still down at his ankles. He also could feel that his legs were spread at the knees. He could feel something very cold and solid against the inside of each knee. In that position, his waist was slightly off the ground, and the tip of his dangling penis touched the cold, wet grass.

Ted turned his head to the left. On the ground was the cattle prod and a long, thin wooden object rounded at the end. He turned his head toward his feet as much as he could and saw the object was a broom. He was certain what the cattle prod was for. But why would someone bring a broom?

While he pondered the possibilities, he could hear the shadow walking around the clearing behind him. He could not get his head around enough to see what it was doing. But he could hear what sounded to him like someone packing something into or unpacking from a container. Or it could have been both.

Suddenly, the noises stopped, and the night was quiet again, except for a light breeze rustling through the treetops, the gentle burbling of the river in the canyon below the clearing, and the hooting of an owl in the distance.

The quiet was starting to give Ted confidence his tormentor had given up and his ordeal was over. He pulled a little harder with his arms in hopes of breaking free then heard some footsteps coming toward him to the left. He saw the boots of the shadow come to a stop on the other side of the broom.

A brown clad hand reached down and picked up the broom. Ted heard what sounded like the lid of a jar being removed. The smell of Vaseline filled his nostrils, and he heard the distinctive squishy sound of something being inserted into the ointment. All of a sudden, things started clicking in his brain, and he began pulling his arms down and tried to bring his knees together.

He felt a boot slam into his left side and, a moment later, felt the cattle prod touch his left butt cheek. When it was triggered, he went slack, even though the shadow kept the electricity going for what seemed like a longer time than any of the other instances.

The next thing Ted felt was a gloved hand on his cheek and it being spread outward. Then he felt the gooey in his butt crack. There was something hard under the goo, and it probed up and down until it found his anus and began to push forward. He tried to squeeze it shut, but the numbness caused by the cattle prod would not let his muscles respond.

The broom handle slid roughly in about an inch, and Ted felt the gloved hand leave his cheek. He then felt another push on the broom handle, and it slid farther into his rectum. It was an odd feeling, almost like the prostate exam he had done recently, but a little more painful as the broom handle was larger than a doctor's finger.

The shadow pushed even harder on the broom handle, and it moved further into the canal. The sensation under other circumstances might have been pleasant. Ted had always wondered what it felt like from a woman's perspective to be penetrated. A part of his mind was saying, *Ah, so that's how it feels.*

At that instant, the Vaseline that had spread from the first inch of the tip along the shaft as it entered his ass ran out, and he felt the rough wood. Then a splinter entered his skin.

"Ow, fuck!" he screamed into the gag.

He didn't have time to completely process that pain because the shadow gave one last thrust to the broom handle, and it traveled another couple of inches. Ted felt intense pain as tender flesh in his anal canal was torn. He bit down on the gag, and his eyes watered.

Then he felt the broom handle making a reverse journey, and as he felt it exit his sore anus, he also felt a warm liquid sensation mix with the gooey Vaseline left on his skin. The liquid dripped down on his balls.

The pain inside him was so intense he felt woozy and his vision started to blur. He could feel himself drifting into unconsciousness again. Then he heard the pop of another smelling salts capsule.

Again, Ted was awake. He felt the shadow turning him over, and he tried to resist by lifting his legs. But he couldn't get them more than a few inches off the ground because he was so weak. For good measure, the shadow gave him a backhanded smack on the back of his head, and it drove his face into the ground.

The shadow rolled him over on his back. The move eased the pain on his belly wounds, but he could still feel warm liquid leaking from his ass. Whatever was damaged by the broom handle was still bleeding. And judging by the flow, it was bleeding heavily. That explained his weakness.

The shadow walked around him and picked up what looked to Ted like a two-by-four about four feet long. He could do nothing but lie there and watch as the shadow walked a full circle around him and stopped at his knees. The shadow took a step back and placed the edge of the board on his right leg halfway between the knee and the ankle. The gloved hands adjusted their grip on the other end of the board.

The board slowly raised above the shadow's head where it paused for a full second then came crashing down on his leg. The pain of the impact was intense, and Ted cried out and bit hard on the gag. Unsatisfied, the shadow raised the board again, paused a second, then swung it downward with a visibly increased effort.

This time, Ted not only felt the pain of the impact but also heard a snap.

The shadow circled to his other leg, laid the board on his leg in roughly the same spot as the other one, and drew back the board and took a swing. This time, it took three whacks before Ted heard the snap of his tibia. With each successive blow, Ted's cries became fainter as the increased pain was sapping what energy he had left.

The shadow moved up to his outstretched arms and took aim on his left forearm. Again, the board was drawn over the masked head and brought down with heavy force. The loud pop on the first swing confirmed to Ted that his arm was broken. He could also feel the cold air on the open would where the bone had torn away the flesh and protruded out.

He lay there whimpering and waited for the shadow to finish the job on his other arm and possibly even his head. He was in such pain he was silently hoping whoever it was would split his skull open and put him out of his misery. He no longer cared who it was who was doing this to him and why.

But no more blows came. He was vaguely aware of the shadow gathering up its tools and shoving them into what sounded like a canvas duffel bag. It then came over to him and cut the ropes securing his feet together. But his pants and underwear were left where they were. The shadow then cut the ropes that tied his hands together and to the tree. The shadow gathered up the ropes and put them in the container.

He followed the figure as it picked up the bag and carried it toward the sound of the river about one hundred feet below. At the edge of a nearly sheer cliff covered in moss, the shadow swung the bag in a horizontal arc and let it fly. After a very short period, Ted heard a splash above the sound of the fast-moving water.

The shadow then walked over and knelt down at his left side, leaning over him so that the dark head was just inches from his face. The shadow hovered there for a moment, then the gloved hands went to the bottom of the mask and lifted it up to expose the face.

Ted stared in astonishment, not sure if he was hallucinating. He knew that face, and he knew it well. But he wasn't ready to believe it. The shadow reached down and untied the gag and removed it from his mouth, the corners of which were raw and bleeding.

When the mask was raised, Ted saw a look of fulfillment on the face of his attacker. The look became even more satisfied by the stunned look on his face.

The shadow said something slowly to him with a smile that had a hint of sadness.

It was the only thing the shadow had said all night. The figure stood, turned on its heel, and walked out of the clearing.

Now the events of the evening were clear as day for Ted. As he tried, with his last reserves of energy, to crawl toward the road, he replayed the events of the attack on Sherry back in his mind. He then replayed the events of this night. The similarities were striking, even as he could feel unconsciousness beginning to overtake him.

The last image and sound he heard in his life was the face of the shadow leaning over him, saying, "Now you know how it felt."

Chapter 21

Barry sat at his small desk in the third-floor room at Hunt Hall on the Eastern Oregon State College campus, textbooks and notebooks full of handwritten notes open in front of him.

He had awoken early that morning without his alarm. He had hoped to sleep in a bit more, but when his eyes fluttered open and he saw the digital numbers on the clock/radio read 6:17, he found that he could not go back to sleep. Ten minutes later, he slowly crawled out of bed and headed for the communal showers.

After a quick wash just to get the night sweat off his body, he went back to his room and quickly dressed in jeans, a T-shirt, and tennis shoes. He took the stairs to the main lobby and exited the building and headed west across campus. His destination was Hoke College Center, or "Choke" as it was referred to by students, where the cafeteria was located. He wanted to fill up on breakfast for the day of studying he anticipated.

As he passed between Ackerman Hall to his right and the brand-new Zabel Hall to his left, he wished he had put on a jacket. The temperature was just flirting with the forties, but the breeze coming in off the Blue Mountains cut to the bone.

It had been a busy week. Having missed classes Monday and Tuesday to be with Sherry during the court sessions in Stevenson, he had been working late into the night all week deciphering the notes several friends had taken in his various classes. It was easy to figure out his own notes, since he had his own version of shorthand and he understood the "code" he used. But others were different in the way they took notes. By Thursday, he had them all figured out, and he planned to spend the morning committing them to memory and reconciling it with what was in textbooks before he left for Carson.

He had lucked out and had the room to himself for the day. His roommate, a fellow freshman, was from Baker, just forty-five miles southeast of the campus, and went home most weekends. For this weekend, he had no classes on Friday, so he drove to Baker the night before.

After breakfast, Barry jogged back to Hunt Hall to cut the time he spent in the breezy cold.

He had been so absorbed in his studies he had no idea what time it was when he heard a loud knocking on his dorm room door. He glanced at the clock/radio and saw 2:33 displayed there. At that instant, his stomach growled. It might have been grumbling for some time, but he was so intent on his work he would not have noticed.

"Damn, I missed lunch," he said out loud.

He had also hoped to be on the road by now. He was sure Sherry was expecting him to arrive earlier in the afternoon. Barry made a mental note to call her as soon as he got rid of whoever was at the door to explain why he was still in La Grande.

He walked to the door and yanked it open, expecting to see one or more of his friends wanting to come in and chat or drag him off on some adventure. He was visibly startled when he saw two Union County Sheriff's Department deputies standing in the hallway.

"Are you Barry Walker?" the tall blond-haired deputy with Tanner on his name tag asked.

"Yes," Barry answered. He was gripped with a bit of panic, and it showed because the other deputy named Smith picked up on it right away.

"Is something wrong?" Smith asked suspiciously.

"I don't know," Barry answered. "Are you hear about Sherry?"

Knowing that Ted had been released from jail, all kinds of scenarios raced through his head. None of them were good.

"Who is Sherry?" Smith asked.

"My girlfriend in Carson, Washington," Barry said, a bit confused. "There's a guy over there who raped and beat her, but he got released from jail, and he might have gone after her again."

"Are you talking about Ted Brennen?" Smith asked.

Barry nodded, not sure what to say.

"He hasn't done anything to anyone," Smith said. "We have some questions for you. May we come in?"

Barry's confusion deepened. If they weren't here about Sherry, what was this all about? He'd had no brushes with law enforcement since coming to La Grande. In fact, there had been none his entire life. But his curiosity was biting at him like a badger on its prey. He stepped aside and motioned for them to enter.

Tanner went to the extremely organized desk of Barry's roommate and pulled out the chair and sat down while his partner sat on the bed on Barry's side of the room, moving the unmade blankets so he was not sitting on the white sheets. Barry sat at his desk.

"Can you account for your whereabouts the last three days?" Tanner asked.

"I have been to all my classes and studying at night," Barry said. "On Monday and Tuesday, I was in Stevenson and Carson. I was there to be with Sherry when this guy Ted had a court hearing."

"And when you weren't in class?" Smith asked.

Barry thought back to refresh his memory.

"Well, at night I've been studying," he said. "I missed two days early in the week, and I'm trying to catch up."

"And where were you while studying?" Tanner asked.

"Mostly here," Barry explained. "Tuesday night, I was at the library because my roommate had friends over and it was too loud to concentrate."

"Can your roommate verify the times you were here and the activity Tuesday night?" Tanner asked. "How can we reach him?"

Barry nodded and explained about his roommate's weekend trip home. He wrote down his parents' phone number on a pad and handed it to Smith. They then asked for names and contact information for his professors in all the classes he had attended during the week. He wrote the information on another piece of paper and gave it to the deputy.

"Can I ask what this is about?" Barry asked.

The deputies stood in unison, almost as if they had practiced the move many times.

"We are collecting information for the Skamania County Sheriff's Department," Tanner said. "Ted Brennen is dead."

When they reached the opened the door and walked into the hallway, the two deputies, again in what appeared to be rehearsed parade moves, turned to face Barry, still sitting at his desk.

"Thank you for your cooperation," Smith said, and they turned and walked down the hallway.

Barry slowly got up and went to the door, poked his head out, and did not see the officers. When he heard the door at the bottom of the stairwell shut, he raced to the pay phone in the middle of the hall.

The phone on the wall in the Dyke home jangled four times before Mary picked it up.

"Is Sherry there?" she heard Barry's voice ask excitedly.

Shortly, Sherry picked the receiver up off the counter and put it to her ear.

"Hello."

"Are you okay?" Barry asked, concern evident in his voice.

"I'm fine," Sherry answered. "You sound worried. What's the matter? Are you on your way?"

"I got a visit from two sheriff's deputies. They just left," Barry said, speaking so fast his words were blending together. He took a breath and continued. "At first, I thought something had happened to you. Maybe that bastard Ted went after you again."

"No, the truth is—"

"And then they told me he is dead," Barry interrupted her. "What the hell happened?"

"The deputies were here a couple of hours ago," Sherry said calmly. She then related to him what took place in their home.

* * *

Deputies Whisnofski and Pyle stood on the porch when Katrina opened the door. Their serious look told her this was not a social call.

"Is your husband at home?" Pyle asked.

"He worked some overtime yesterday, so he's still asleep," she said.

"Could you wake him, please?" Pyle asked.

Katrina could tell by the tone of his voice and the look in his eye that while it was phrased as a question, the deputy expected compliance.

"All right, you can wait for him there," she said despite the chilly weather, and she shut the door in their faces.

The two deputies looked at each other. This was out of character for the woman they had come to know in the last few months. She had always been so polite, so welcoming. But her attitude was something they had seen before from people who expected justice from the court system and were disappointed with the result. Those people felt betrayed and angry. The deputies were sure Katrina Dyke was feeling the same.

With that in mind, neither officer took personal offense. After all, they knew the feelings of betrayal and anger, especially in this case.

They had been standing in the cold wind, with little protection against its bite despite their heavy leather jackets, for about five minutes before the door opened. Bob stood there. He said nothing.

"Mr. Dyke, we'd like to ask you a few questions," Whisnofski said. "May we come in?"

"Go ahead and ask your questions," Bob said, still standing in the doorway and making no welcoming motion.

He's pissed too, Whisnofski thought to himself.

"Well, I don't mind saying it's a little chilly out here, so if you would like, we can talk in our vehicle," Whisnofski said, trying not to sound irritated.

Bob, saying nothing, reached to his left to retrieve his jacket and threw it on as he walked out the door, following the officers to the Crown Victoria still running at the edge of the street. Pyle directed Bob into the front passenger seat and climbed into the back seat

GORGE JUSTICE

behind him while Whisnofski walked around and climbed into the driver's seat. Once a moment of silence passed, in which Whisnofski reached up and adjusted the rearview mirror, he turned to Bob, who was staring out the windshield.

"There has been a development," Whisnofski said. "Ted Brennen is dead."

From the back seat, Pyle could see Bob's face in the adjusted mirror. There was a second or two of noncomprehension then a look of satisfaction.

"If you're expecting me to say I'm sorry to hear that, you'll be disappointed," Bob said, still staring straight ahead.

"Be that as it may, can you tell us where you were in the last couple of days?" the deputy in the driver's seat asked.

"Working at the mill all week," Bob said. "I worked a few hours over my regular shift yesterday."

"What about at night?" Whisnofski asked.

"Supper and a little TV with my family and then sleep," Bob said, his tone softening a little bit. "Except last night, since it was a little late for anything after a late dinner."

"And I suppose your family will verify all that," Whisnofski said.

"Yes, and you can check the time cards at the mill for the work hour," Bob said.

"We will do that," Whisnofski said. "We'll start with your family. Can you send your wife out here so we can talk to her?"

Bob sat unchanged in stature for a second or two. He then turned to Pyle in the back seat then to Whisnofski.

"We have been through a lot in the last couple of years, and it has been very wearing on all of us," he said. "And then when…" He paused, catching himself before saying what he wanted to about Ted. He then continued, "When the court let that guy go, we lost all faith in the justice system."

"We understand, Mr. Dyke," Pyle put in before Bob could continue. "Believe me, we are as disappointed as you are."

Bob wanted to say there was no way they could be anywhere near as disappointed as he and his family were, especially Sherry. But he bit his tongue.

"What I'm trying to say is, I want you to continue your questioning inside our home," Bob said. "We really don't want you to feel unwelcome."

When they entered the house, Katrina was in the kitchen and shot the deputies a sour look and a questioning one to Bob. He asked the deputies to wait there and went to speak to his wife. The officers saw him speak to her, and her hand went to her mouth. She did not say a word during the brief conversation. Bob then motioned for the deputies to come in and have a seat at the dining table.

"How do you want to do this?" Bob asked.

"I think it would be easier if we could talk to everyone at once," Pyle said. Bob then went to the stairs and called the children downstairs. When they were gathered around him, he briefed them in a quiet voice. They all took a seat around the table.

"As I'm sure Mr. Dyke has told you all, Ted Brennen is dead," Whisnofski said. "It was under circumstances that indicate foul play, so we need to account for all your whereabouts in the last couple of days."

He looked around the table and settled on Katrina.

"I was working at the diner during the days, and then I was home after that," she said.

"And at night?" Pyle asked.

"Asleep," she answered then added before she was asked, "with my husband."

"Is there any way he could have sneaked out while you were asleep?" Pyle asked, trying to be as businesslike as possible.

"We are both light sleepers, so if either of us got up at night, the other would wake up," she said. Katrina neglected to say that the exception to that was, after they have sex, they both sleep more deeply. But with all the children present, she didn't think it necessary to share that detail.

Sherry told the deputies she had spent the days at home doing household chores for her mother and making a few calls to Eastern Oregon State College about admission for the next academic year. She provided the admissions office number and the person's name whom she spoke to each time. During the evening, she was with the family, and at night, she was asleep in the room she shared with Mary.

Her younger sister was in school, spent Thursday afternoon watching her brother's football practice, and then was home with the family.

Ralph's school activities and football practice occupied his days and the family activities in the evening.

There was silence for a moment, then Kim spoke up.

"I was in school and then home," she said.

Pyle and Whisnofski looked at each other and then back to her. They had already eliminated her as a suspect since she was too small to have been able to overpower Ted. Nor did they think her capable of the things that were done to him. But they admired her for speaking up.

"We'll check your school to make sure," Pyle said, which put a smile on her face, feeling like she, too, was part of the discussion. "And we'll verify everyone else's information," he added more seriously.

The two deputies began to stand, but Bob halted them with a question.

"You said foul play was suspected," he said. "What exactly happened to him?"

"Well, we can't talk about specific details since it is an ongoing investigation, but it appears he was taken against his will and beaten pretty badly."

"How badly?" Sherry asked.

The deputies looked at her deeply, trying to define her intent in asking. But her face was a blank slate.

"All we can say is, his injuries were similar to yours," Pyle said.

"How similar?" she asked.

"Let's just say very similar," Whisnofski said.

They searched all the faces for any kind of reaction that might give them a clue whether any of them were involved. But there was nothing, except that same look of satisfaction Bob had in the car when he first heard of Ted's death.

* * *

Barry took in her narrative without interruption. He was still trying to process his visit with the Union County deputies and the fact that with Ted's death, the threat to Sherry was now gone.

When Sherry finished, questions were swimming through his mind.

"What happened to him?" he asked.

"They didn't give us many details, but someone took him out and beat him to death," Sherry answered.

Neither one felt any sympathy for Ted. Instead, they shared a feeling of relief.

"So why are they talking to your family about it?" he asked. "Do they think one of you did it?"

"Maybe," Sherry said. "But no one in my family would have done something like this."

Barry recalled their conversation in the little red diner. He wanted to remind her that they had talked about doing the very thing that had transpired. He was certain Sherry would not have acted on those plans without him. But he wondered whether her father would have.

But he dared not talk about what they had discussed. He didn't want to upset Sherry, and he did not want anyone overhearing what they had talked about.

"I'm sure they have to check all possibilities," Barry said. "That's why they had the deputies over here talk to me."

For a long pause, there was silence between them. Sherry finally broke it.

"Barry, the cops said he had injuries similar to mine," she said hesitantly. "They said very similar."

"What do you think that means?" he asked.

"I think whoever did it wanted him to feel what I felt," she said. "Just like I wanted, just like we both wanted."

Barry thought about that for a moment before responding.

"Did you talk to anyone else about that?" he asked.

"Just Karen," she said.

"Do you think she did it or had someone do it?" Barry asked.

"I don't think she would," Sherry said. "But I don't really know for sure."

Again, there was a short period of silence.

"Well, I wouldn't worry about it," Barry said. "The bastard is dead. You have nothing to worry about, and none of us were involved."

Sherry reveled in the confidence he had in her and her family that they were not involved in so vile an act, no matter how satisfying that act was to her.

Chapter 22

Deputies Whisnofski and Pyle spent Saturday interviewing the Dyke family then following the leads they discovered the day before at the clearing where Ted's body was found. But those leads were slim.

The body had been discovered Friday afternoon by a Carson resident who was traveling up the adjacent road. He was driving the road to test out a new front end he installed in his 1965 Ford pickup. As he drove by the clearing, he caught a glimpse of what he thought was an animal lying on the ground.

He stopped and walked toward it. He had gotten halfway there when he realized it was a human body. He started to move to it then noticed something peculiar about the body. He got back in his truck and drove straight to the nearest business and called the sheriff's office.

Bloodstains on the grass pointed investigators to the tree just a few feet away. There, they found traces of rope fibers. Imprints on the grass and the dirt at the base of the tree indicated he had been sitting then lying, or vice versa, adjacent to the tree. But that was not where he was found.

The body was on its belly about ten feet from the bloodstained grass with the head pointing toward the road. It appeared to be that he had tried to crawl out of the clearing, but his energy gave out.

Because they had investigated Sherry's attack in the same clearing, Whisnofski and Pyle were called out to look over the scene after an initial inspection by the officer first on the scene.

"His pants and underwear are pulled down around his ankles," Whisnofski said as he knelt beside the body. "You suppose that happened while he was trying to crawl?"

Pyle walked around the body, looking closely at the ground around and behind it. He then knelt on the opposite side from Whisnofski and gently rolled the body and inspected the front of the bare legs and the groin.

"I don't think so," he said. "The scratching and staining look like these areas were bare from the start of the crawl."

With a gloved hand, he moved the penis to look at both sides.

"There are burn marks on both sides of his cock," Pyle said. "Could be electrical burns."

Pyle let the body roll back onto the ground.

"We'll need to wait for the coroner's report, but I'm leaning toward him having been tortured in some way," Pyle said. "Did this guy have any identification on him?" he asked the deputy who was the first law enforcement officer in the clearing.

"Nothing," he responded.

Whisnofski and Pyle moved to where the head was turned partially to one side and knelt down to look at the face.

"You know who that is?" Pyle asked his partner.

Whisnofski recognized him from the court hearing and initial arrest and interrogation.

"That is Ted Brennen," he said.

Whisnofski and Pyle spent Sunday with their families and Monday conducting follow-up interviews with the Dyke family. Early Tuesday morning, they met in the briefing room at the Stevenson station to compare notes.

Monday's follow-up interviews with the Dykes were very much the same as the original ones during the weekend. Kim, Ralph, and Mary had been interviewed at their schools after their parents gave their consent to allow the deputies to talk to them without their presence.

"We have nothing to hide, and we trust our children," Bob had said when asked permission to interview the children at school. "They were not involved in this."

With their notes and other related documents and evidence spread before them on the small conference table, Whisnofski and Pyle were uncertain in what direction the investigation should take.

"So what are you thinking?" Whisnofski asked his partner.

Pyle shuffled through his notes, scanning the handwritten words, then poured over a couple of documents before answering.

"Well, the fact that he was clearly tortured, especially shoving something up his ass, and his other injuries are almost exactly the same as Sherry Dyke's, I'd say the motive was certainly some type of sick vigilante justice," Pyle said, looking at the details on the preliminary coroner's report.

"Which means we have a slew of suspects, all of whom have very strong motive," Whisnofski said.

He looked around among the papers spread before him and picked up an overnight delivery envelope and removed a letter.

"We can cross the boyfriend off the suspect list," he told Pyle. "I got this from Union County late yesterday. They confirmed with all his professors and several witness interviews that Barry Walker was in La Grande all week."

Pyle flipped through his notes, settling on several pages.

"Cross off the older Dyke brother and Sherry's friend Karen," he said. "University of Puget Sound professors and her roommate said Karen never left campus, and Terry Dyke was accounted for either on duty or on base all week."

"That leaves us with Sherry herself and the rest of her immediately family," Whisnofski said, leaning back in the metal folding chair with the padded seat and back. "And they all seem to have alibis."

Pyle rested his elbows on the table and placed his chin in his upturned cupped hands.

"Why do I get the feeling you doubt one, some, or all of those alibis?" he said.

Whisnofski shook his head and sighed.

"Taken at face value, they seem rock solid," he said. "We can account without question for all their whereabouts during the day."

"But...?" Pyle said.

"But what about at night?" Whisnofski said. "They are basically alibiing one another. That means any of them, or a combination of them, could have snuck out at night and done the deed."

He reached over and grabbed the coroner's preliminary report.

"The coroner believes the time of death is sometime between ten o'clock Thursday night and three o'clock Friday morning," he said.

"So who do you think is capable of things like that?" Pyle asked, indicating the coroner's report.

Whisnofski glanced over the description of the condition of Ted's body and his conclusions.

"He thinks the burn marks on his body were made by a cattle prod," he said. "The limb breaks were such that they were made by a blunt object. My guess is, someone whaled away on them until they broke."

He paused a moment and reread a section of the report.

"That object up the ass is pretty extreme," he said, "I think whoever did this somehow wanted him to know what it felt like to be raped, like Sherry was."

Pyle suddenly sat up and searched through his notes, opening the notebook to one page, and shuffled through the documents before finding notes he had taken during a conversation with Deputy Benjamin Waverly from Pierce County Sheriff's Department.

"When I talked to Waverly up in Pierce County about his interview with Sherry's friend Karen, she told him Sherry had told her once that she wanted Ted to feel exactly what she felt in her attack."

He then turned to his own notebook.

"And yesterday, I was at the diner where Katrina Dyke works, and some guy caught me in the parking lot and told me he overheard Sherry and Barry Walker talking about what they would do to Ted if they could," he explained. "What they talked about sounds a lot like what actually happened."

Whisnofski, still leaning back in his chair, put his hands on his head and looked thoughtful for a few moments.

"Just because of those discussions, I'd have to say Sherry is a strong suspect," he finally said. "But without her boyfriend to help, would she be able to do it alone…and I mean emotionally as well as physically?"

"I don't know. If properly motivated, I think most people can do things you wouldn't expect," Pyle said.

They sat in silence for a few long minutes. Whisnofski looked over another document that reported the DeSoto Ted had bought in Stevenson was found next to his apartment in Home Valley. It also detailed information about the note left for the apartment manager saying he would be leaving Friday.

"He was getting ready to leave Washington," Whisnofski said. "Do you suppose whoever did that to him got wind that he was leaving and acted on impulse?"

"This seems planned to me," Pyle said.

Again, they sat in silence, looking over the documents in front of them.

"So where does that leave us?" Pyle finally said.

"Well, based on our interactions with him, I'd say the father is the most motivated to get revenge for his daughter," Whisnofski said. "Sherry certainly had motivation, but she does not strike me as the type to do the things that were done to him."

"Could the father have snuck out and done it without his wife knowing, or is she covering for him?" Pyle asked.

"Or did they do it together?" Whisnofski asked.

Pyle threw his hands out to either side with the palms of his hands up in a gesture of puzzlement.

It was at that moment that Deputy Allen Kline poked his head in the room.

"There are two guys out front wanting to talk to the deputies investigating the Ted Brennen case," he said. "You're going to want to hear them out."

The two deputies walked into the interview room and found two men seated on the same side of a table on bare metal folding chairs. They were dressed like most workingmen in the Columbia River communities, blue jeans with heavy work boots and flannel long-sleeve shirts buttoned up the front. One could be described as average-looking; he had straight blond hair stuffed under a John Deere baseball cap. The other had brown hair and a rough-skinned face with several moles scattered around it.

Both seemed to be in their midtwenties and reasonably physically fit. They looked to be mill workers. They also looked very nervous.

"So you boys have something you want to talk to us about?" Whisnofski asked, remaining standing.

"We need your protection," the blonde said.

Whisnofski looked at Pyle with a questioning look. His partner pulled a rolling desk chair from against the wall and sat down opposite the pair at the table. Whisnofski stayed on his feet, despite the fact there were two metal chairs folded, and leaned against the wall.

"Just what would we be protecting you from?" Pyle asked.

"We don't know," the blonde said.

Pyle looked over his shoulder at Whisnofski. He could tell by his partner's expression they were thinking the same thing. The man was being truthful to an extent, but he knew more than he was volunteering.

"So then tell us why you need protection," Pyle said.

"It has to do with a rape and beating of a girl," the blonde said.

Suddenly, the interest level for both deputies shot up. Whisnofski grabbed one of the metal chairs, unfolded it, and sat next to Pyle.

"Let's start with your names," he said, taking out the notepad and pencil from his uniform shirt pocket.

"I'm Sam Bodine, and this is Kenny Sanders," the blonde said. It was not lost on the deputies that only he had spoken so far.

"Who is this girl who was raped and attacked?" Whisnofski asked.

"Her name is Sherry," Bodine said. "It was in the newspapers."

"What do the two of you have to do with that?" Pyle asked.

"We were there when it happened, but neither of us raped her nor beat her up," Bodine said hurriedly. "But we know who did it."

"And who was that?" Pyle asked.

"We need to know we'll be protected," Bodine said. "If we say, something bad could happen to us."

"Why would you be in any danger if you didn't have anything to do with the girl's attack?" Whisnofski asked.

"Because it was Ted Brennen who did it," Sanders blurted out. Bodine gave him an angry look.

"Dammit, Kenny, I told you not to say anything until they agreed to protect us!" he yelled.

Pyle held up a hand, palm outward.

"Wait a minute. You do know Ted Brennen is dead. That was in the newspapers too," he said. "So there's nothing he can do to you."

"Yeah, but whoever killed him can," Sanders said. Again, he got an angry look from his cohort.

Pyle got up and left the room. Whisnofski decided to halt the questions until his partner returned, which he did shortly with two legal pads and pens. He placed one of each in front of the two men then sat back down.

"Write down everything you know about Sherry's rape and attack," Pyle said, deliberately omitting her last name.

"We met this guy Ted at the mill, and we partied together," Bodine said quickly. "Then he told us about this girl. He said they did role-playing games."

"Just write down everything and sign at the bottom," Whisnofski said.

"Are you going to arrest us?" Sanders asked.

"Depends on what you write," he answered. Then both deputies left the room, having another officer wait inside the room to collect their statements.

* * *

Sherry got into Barry's Grand Prix early on a Saturday morning, and they headed down the road toward the Columbia River. It was overcast, and light rain was forecast for the day. The young couple was going to Portland to do a little shopping. Christmas was a bit more than a month away, and they had gifts to purchase.

Barry had driven home from La Grande the night before, stopping in Carson to visit Sherry and her family briefly. Sherry suggested the shopping trip.

But she had another motive. While making their way to the freeway, they chitchatted about everyday things, updating each other on their activities, such as they were, since they had seen each other less than a week previously.

After settling into the light I-80 westbound traffic, Sherry got to the real reason she wanted to be alone with Barry.

"I'm a little worried about this investigation into Ted's death," she said.

It caught Barry off guard, and he didn't respond right away, driving in silence for about a mile.

"What are you worried about?" he finally asked.

"Well, what we talked about that day in the diner," she answered.

He thought for a moment, replaying the conversation in his mind.

"We talked about what we would like to do to Ted for what he did to you," he said. "I don't think that's anything to worry about."

"But we talked about doing some terrible things," she said.

"People who have been through what you have would naturally want to get even, especially when you get no justice from the courts," Barry said, letting his frustration about that lack of justice in this case show.

"But I think the cops suspect my family or I had something to do with it," she said.

"How can you be sure about that?" he asked.

"I don't know. It just seemed like some of the questions they asked made it seem that way," Sherry said.

They were silent again for a while. The traffic on the freeway began to increase as they got closer to Troutdale, a small eastern suburb of Portland. Barry knew it would get busier as they got closer to the center of the metro area. He did not want to spend this trip talking about negative things like Ted's death.

"You didn't do it, and I'm sure no one in your family would do something like that," he said, "even if they really wanted to."

Sherry moved closer to him and put her hand on his thigh. She was thankful to have someone in her life who was so supportive, loving, and caring. She wondered how she could be so lucky.

No more was said about Ted or his death for the rest of the trip. They spent the morning at Lloyd Center then had lunch and some final shopping at Jantzen Beach. They talked almost nonstop about their future, including the near future that would see Sherry heading to La Grande the next fall to begin her college education.

When the afternoon was nearly over and they were close to home, they saw a sight that was so compelling they had to extend their trip. After leaving the freeway, Barry steered the car not onto the Bridge of the Gods approach but into Cascade Locks, the small town across the river from Stevenson. They went to a small park overlooking the river and the locks that were built to help river traffic bypass the Cascades Rapids before Bonneville Dam was built and made them unnecessary.

They sat on a bench and looked north at the most striking rainbow across the now-clear sky they had ever seen. The arching prism included every shade in the color spectrum, and unlike most rainbows, the transition between colors was stark, not blurred. The rainbow stretched from the Rooster Rock area to the west with its eastern end seeming to come down right in the middle of where Carson would be.

Sherry looked at it in awe. While she did not believe in the old Irish folktale of a pot of gold at the end of a rainbow, she believed it was a beacon of hope and a good fortune.

Chapter 23

Sitting in Barry's car outside her home, the couple looked at each in silence for a few minutes. Neither wanted to say anything to break the mood of their trip to Portland. Aside from the early conversation, it had been an uplifting day, and they wanted to preserve that.

"I really enjoyed our day together," Barry finally said, choosing his words carefully.

"Me too," she answered. She leaned in closer to him and gave him a long, soft kiss. "I can't wait to start our lives together."

"We have started that life together," Barry said. "I love you, Sherry, and I want to spend the rest of my life with you."

She threw her arms around him and squeezed tightly.

"Is that a proposal?" she asked teasingly.

"It's a promise, but you call it what you want," he said into her soft hair.

Just as the words left his mouth, he saw Bob Dyke come out the front door and stand on the porch, looking their way. Their intimate closeness did not embarrass him or make him feel threatened by her father's attention. Barry knew Bob was aware of how they felt for each other, and he seemed very comfortable with it.

But the look of concern on Bob's face gave Barry pause, and he pulled away from Sherry's embrace. She was puzzled, but when she saw Barry looking past her, she turned her head and saw her father standing there.

"Something's wrong," she said and reached for the door latch. Barry exited the car immediately and joined Sherry as she headed up the front walk.

"What's up, Dad?" she asked as she stepped in front of her father.

"We had another visit from the sheriff's deputies," he answered.

* * *

Whisnofski and Pyle got out of the car and walked reluctantly up the walk to the Dykes' front door. Over the months since Sherry Dyke was attacked and they were assigned the case, they had gotten to know this family.

They had grown to like them, and in the days since Ted Brennen's body was discovered, they had leaned toward the conclusion that none of the Dykes had anything to do with his death.

But as law enforcement officers, they had to face the facts they had been able to gather. Everyone they had investigated as possible suspects had airtight alibis. While each of the Dyke family members had alibis, there was some doubt for the parents and the older children at home. The deputies could not ignore the possibility that the Dykes were covering for one another. Any one or a combination of them could have committed the crime.

Based on the coroner's description of Ted's burn wounds, they had another lead to check out. So it was with a heavy heart that they knocked on the Dykes' front door.

Kim opened the door to the deputies. She immediately turned her head toward the kitchen.

"The cops are here again," she said. The deputies couldn't help but detect a hint of distaste in her voice when she uttered the word *cops*.

Within seconds, Bob was at the door.

"What is it this time?" he asked. That same hint of distaste was in his voice.

"We are sorry to disturb you again, Mr. Dyke, but we would like to search your house and property," Whisnofski said, trying to keep his tone neutral.

"What for?" Bob asked.

"We will be looking for anything that might be connected with Ted Brennen's death," Pyle said.

"I'll be a son of a bitch. You think one of us is involved in this," Bob said, the anger rising in his voice. Kim, who had remained at the door, turned and ran up the stairs, calling for her mother.

"Mr. Dyke, please calm down," Pyle said. "It's also possible that we'll find nothing, and that could clear you all."

"I don't think I like strangers going through our personal belongings," Bob said, easing his tone a bit, but still angry at the implication of a search. "If you tell me what you're looking for, I can tell you we don't have it."

"Mr. Dyke, we would like to do this with your consent," Whisnofski said as he reached into his inside jacket pocket and pulled out a trifold piece of paper. "But if we have to, we'll invoke this search warrant."

Bob rolled his eyes as Katrina and the rest of the family, minus Sherry who was with Barry on their shopping trip, came barreling down the stairs.

"Since we don't really have a choice, go right ahead," Bob said sarcastically, sweeping his left hand out toward the inside of the home in a mock welcoming gesture.

Pyle turned and motioned with his hand to a car parked behind theirs, and two more deputies got out and came toward the house.

"You two search the yards, and we'll look inside," he instructed, then he and Whisnofski went in the house.

Bob, Katrina, and the children sat in the living room while the search was undertaken. Bob explained what was going on.

"What are they looking for?" Ralph asked.

"I don't know. They wouldn't say," his father answered.

While they listened to noise from upstairs of dresser drawers being pulled out, rummaged through, then replaced; closet doors opening then closing after a short period; and even the toilet tank lids being taken off then replaced, they kept quiet. No one wanted to speculate while the deputies were in the house.

Shortly, Whisnofski and Pyle came downstairs and continued their search through the kitchen drawers and cabinets, the laundry room, and the front closet. Pyle then asked them to stand, and the deputies searched the furniture.

Without a word to the Dykes, the deputies then exited the home through the back door. Bob went to the kitchen window and watched the four officers in a discussion. Then the two deputies who had gotten out of the other car returned to the vehicle and drove away.

Bob saw Whisnofski and Pyle come toward the house, and he went back to his family. The deputies returned to the house through the back door and addressed the family, still standing in the living room.

"We've completed our search, and we want to thank you for your cooperation," Pyle said.

"What did you find?" Bob asked.

The deputies looked at each other and sighed. Whisnofski nodded.

"We didn't find anything that would be helpful in this investigation," Pyle said.

"So that means we're not suspects?" Bob asked.

There was a short silence. The deputies again looked at each other, an unspoken message passing between them. This time, it was Whisnofski who spoke.

"The reality is, Mr. Dyke," he began then looked at Katrina and the children in turn before going on, "while you all have alibis for the period we believe he was killed, the possibility still exists that one or more of you could be covering for one or more of the others."

Bob started to protest, the anger rising visibly in him, but Whisnofski cut him off.

"That's the way we have to look at it as investigators," he said. "We have to approach it in a neutral way."

He paused, expecting Bob to comment again, but he did not.

"But when I look at it from a personal perspective—and I think I can speak for Deputy Pyle on this—I have come to know you and your family, and I have a hard time believing any of you could have done what was done in that clearing."

No one spoke for a moment, soaking it all in. Then Pyle broke the silence.

"We understand your feelings," he said. "And we're certain you wanted justice for your daughter and sister, but wanting something like this and actually doing it are two different things."

"Does this mean it's over, your investigation?" Ralph asked.

"The case will stay open until we determine who did it," Whisnofski said. "But we have to have solid evidence before we can charge anyone."

Bob stepped up to the deputies and offered his hand. They both took it in turn and shook it.

"Thank you for your openness," he said. "If there is any way we can help, just let us know."

Without another word, the deputies nodded and left the home.

Throughout the search, Katrina had not said a single word.

* * *

Sherry woke early Sunday morning. She felt refreshed after the first full night's sleep she had enjoyed in more than a year. There had been no nightmares of the rape in Wyoming, the rape and beating in Washington, or for the past week, the nightmares of her or other members of her family being arrested and charged in Ted's murder.

Finally, her future looked bright. She had dreamed of going to college, spending more time with Barry and, a bit further in the future, of the two of them marrying and starting a family of their own.

For Sherry Dyke, a new life began that morning.

She threw off the blankets and felt the chill of the winter air, despite the hum of the furnace and the heat blowing out the vent on the other side of the room. She sat on the edge of her bed, letting her body become accustomed to the comparatively cooler temperature than she had enjoyed under the three thick blankets on her bed.

The house was eerily absent of human noises. That meant no one else was up yet. Sherry looked at her alarm clock and saw that it was not yet six o'clock. Despite that, there was a bluish light filtering in through the spaces on either side of her window not entirely covered by the thick curtains.

She padded over to the window and pushed one curtain aside. The edges around the window were crusted with moisture that had frozen and looked like the patterns in crystal vases. But her view through the rest of the glass was unobscured.

The backyard was covered with a pristine layer of snow. It wasn't much, maybe an inch, if that. It was easy to measure by looking at the fifty-five-gallon barrel with the top off at the far end of the yard. The snow barely covered the lip around the bottom where it was fastened to the body of the barrel.

Sherry marveled at the sight for a few minutes. When she had awoken to an overnight snowfall in the past, there were usually some indication of life—small footprints from rabbits, squirrels, and sometimes even deer—that disturbed the new bed of snow every time. But not today. It was a sight she wanted to savor.

Suddenly, out of the corner of her eye to her right, she caught movement. Thinking she might catch the first critters scrabbling through the snow, instead she saw the door of the Baxters' backyard shed open. Emerging from the shed was her mother.

Wearing snow boots, jeans, and a parka, Katrina carried a large cardboard box. Sherry saw no yellow hue on the snow in the Baxters' backyard, meaning no one was stirring there.

Neither the Baxters nor Dykes had their backyards fenced, so Katrina walked straight to the barrel in her backyard. She set the box next to the barrel. Katrina pulled out a large wad of newspapers and dropped them into the barrel.

Transfixed with curiosity, Sherry watched as her mother lit the newspapers with a match then dumped more newspapers on top of the growing flames that began to light up the yard.

Then she pulled a black object that looked like a wool cap. As Katrina held it above the flames, letting them lick the bottom, the light from the fire illuminated what looked like holes in the cap, like eyeholes in a ski mask. One by one, Katrina retrieved items from the box—a faded black sweatshirt and a pair of jeans she recognized as her father's—and ignited them in the same way as the cap.

After watching the fire burn for a few moments, Katrina pulled a plastic jug of lighter fluid from her parka pocket, squirted some on the fire, and watched it flare up. She put the jug back in her pocket and watched the fire for a bit longer. She then threw in a pair of brown gloves, followed by a pair of brown work boots a moment later. Again, she squirted lighter fluid into the fire, and the flames leaped higher briefly then calmed down to a steady burn.

Katrina then used a four-foot piece of rebar to stir the contents of the barrel, sending a shower of sparks into the air. Another squirt of lighter fluid followed and another ten minutes of watching the fire. Katrina then dumped in more newspapers from the box and folded the box itself and pushed it down into the conflagration. More lighter fluid and the fire flared again, only to ease back to its steady flickering.

Sherry was mesmerized. Destroyed flammable items in the barrel was nothing new. It was a common practice in their former home in Wyoming as a way of reducing the amount of trash to haul to the town dump in a community with no municipal curbside sanitation services. It was the same in small towns in Washington, and the Dykes carried on the practice after the move.

But Sherry could not remember a time when burning items in the barrel had ever been done so early in the morning. And why was her mother burning items she took from the Baxters' shed?

She was pondering these inconsistencies when her mother turned and began to walk toward the house. After a few steps, she noticed Sherry watching from her bedroom window. She stopped, and their eyes locked on each other.

Sherry could see a tear rolling down her mother's cheek as she mouthed "I love you" then "I just wanted to protect you."

It was in that moment that Sherry knew she was truly safe.

About the Author

Rusty Bradshaw has been around. He was born in California and grew up in Wyoming. After graduating from Dubois High School, he attended Northwest College in Powell then went to Oregon to obtain his bachelor's degree from Eastern Oregon University. It was in Oregon where Rusty, an avid reader, started what has been a forty-plus-year career in journalism at several newspapers in Seaside, St. Helens, Milton-Freewater, and Astoria. During his career in Oregon, Rusty won several writing awards from the Oregon Newspaper Publishers Association. He was also named Junior Citizen of the Year by the Milton-Freewater Chamber of Commerce and coached youth football for nine years.

Rusty's career continues after a move to Arizona in 2004. He is editor of two newspapers in age-restricted communities—Sun City and Sun City West. He has two grown children—Sara in Oregon and Evan in Idaho. He lives in Glendale with his wife, Jeanne. They enjoy football, casino bingo, road trips, jigsaw puzzles, and any other activities they can do together.

Other books by Rusty Bradshaw:
The Rehabilitation of Miss Little
Moist on the Mountain

CPSIA information can be obtained
at www.ICGtesting.com
Printed in the USA
FSHW010321230921
84925FS